FIRST STEPS TOWARD
CULTURAL DIFFERENCE

Socialization in Infant/Toddler Day Care

FIRST STEPS TOWARD CULTURAL DIFFERENCE

Socialization in Infant/Toddler Day Care

Darla Ferris Miller

Child Welfare League of America

Washington, DC

© 1989 by the Child Welfare League of America, Inc.

All Rights Reserved. Neither this book nor any part may be reproduced or transmitted in any form or by any means, electronic or mechanical, including photocopying, microfilming, and recording, or by any information storage and retrieval system, without permission in writing from the publisher. For information on this or other CWLA publications, contact the CWLA Publications Department at the address below.

CHILD WELFARE LEAGUE OF AMERICA, INC.
440 First Street, NW, Suite 310, Washington, DC 20001-2085

CURRENT PRINTING (last digit)
10 9 8 7 6 5 4 3 2 1

Cover design by Patricia Hopkins
Cover illustrations by Cynde Allyson Miller
Text design by Eve Malakoff-Klein

Printed in the United States of America

ISBN # 0-87868-351-8

Library of Congress Cataloging-in-Publication Data

Miller, Darla Ferris.
    First steps toward cultural difference : socialization in infant/toddler day care / Darla Ferris Miller.
        p. cm.
    Bibliography: p.
    ISBN 0–87868–351–8 (pbk.) : $19.95
    1. Socialization. 2. Day care centers--United States. 3. Social classes--United States.   I. Title.
HQ783.M55 1988
303.3'2--dc19   88–29954
                                                                           CIP

CONTENTS

PREFACE

The use of day care for infants and toddlers across socioeconomic levels has increased dramatically during this decade. Although published research in early socialization outside the home is sparse, folk wisdom and a growing body of work in cognition indicate that environmental factors encountered in the first years of life may facilitate or hinder a child's later success in school and in other social institutions that give one access to power and material resources.

This study is presented as a preliminary description of day care experiences, in a cross-section of socioeconomic levels, of infants and toddlers, and the adults who care for them. It focuses on the verbal and nonverbal social interactions that occur among adults and children during the socialization process, and the accommodation and resistance of very young children to that process.

The study incorporates the qualitative methodology of ethnography for the collection of data through participant observation, in-depth semistructured and structured interviews, still photographs, and audiotape recordings. Three day care centers serving children under three years of age were selected using stratified random selection from cells representing high, middle, and low socioeconomic status. An additional center was added during data analysis to clarify findings. Data were analyzed by means of domain and taxonomic sequences throughout the study.

Socioeconomically based variations uncovered in this study may contribute to social reproduction and therefore have important implications for educational intervention and governmental policy making. Findings of this study are somewhat limited by the small pool of appropriate centers available for sampling.

ACKNOWLEDGMENTS

For their help in the structuring and development of this project, and technical guidance in its conduct, I owe a particular debt to Dr. Mark Ginsburg, Dr. Howard Jones, Dr. Allen Warner, and Dr. Peggy Emerson.

Thanks are due to Dr. Jeanette Phillips for her unfailing support, to Cynde Allyson Miller for her sensitive and precise line drawings, and to Michelle Denise Miller and my husband Tommy Miller for their help in the preparation and writing of the manuscript. I must also thank Margaret Ellison, Myrna Miller, and Karen Ferris Burkhardt. No study could have taken place without the patient willingness of adult and child participants to tolerate interruptions caused by the long hours of observation, audiotaping, and photographing.

I

INTRODUCTION

Ideas about the nature of infancy and childhood cannot be taken for granted. Current views on early childhood are not universal and have not always existed, they are human social inventions, and as such must be examined carefully.

In Western Europe only a century and a half ago, babies were not thought to be real persons. They were treated as property by their parents, and it was not even thought necessary to report their deaths [Aries 1962]. Child care practices have been strikingly different over time for various social classes. A long period of protected childhood has largely been a luxury of the middle and upper classes, and views of infancy have fluctuated according to cultural and class settings [Bremner 1970-1974; Cole 1950; Froebel 1887; Glubok 1969; McGraw 1941; Osborn 1972; Rousseau 1893; Ulich 1954].

Much of the existing literature on child-rearing, infant care, and early day care curriculum seems geared toward some mono-cultural model of optimum care. There is, however, ample evidence that early experiences hold significant cultural importance—that they have dramatic impact on the transformation of the organic, embryonic newborn into a socially complex creature whose written and/or spoken language, intellectual prowess, and social intercourse limit or enhance one's ability to function well in one or another cultural setting.

Socialization practices are a cultural adaptation to accurate or inaccurate perceptions of the structural reality of the social setting. These rationales for child-rearing provide a basis for cultural traditions or legacies and contemporary cultural practices as well as a source of resistance to those same entities. To dig down to the roots of social inequality, one must uncover the subtle beginnings of the social perceptions that legitimate and perpetuate a given social structure.

People from different cultural and economic backgrounds often hold starkly contrasting views about the parameters of proper child care. Child care workers sometimes perceive similar events to have opposite meanings. For example, consider the following statements made by two day care directors:

> I cannot remember any, not any, to my memory, any parents being prepared for the feelings they have when they walk out the door that first time. We have to help them gain confidence that they are not depriving their children in any way, that what they are doing is okay. I would like to see parents come more often during the day. I think they would be more comfortable with, more secure that they are doing the right thing and that they picked the right place. [high-income day care center director, field notes.]

> How did we know this was the right way to take care of babies? Well, we didn't wanta just house 'em. We figured it may not help but it cain't hurt. I been goin' out to the university for three years. I know they say you cain't teach these little babies this stuff—but that's just wrong! This is a great big deal for the parents. They say "Look at what my little baby can do." They're very supportive. [low-income day care center director, field notes.]

As the preceding statements indicate, the process of leaving a very young child in group care was expected by one day care director to evoke guilt in parents and by another to result in feelings of pride. Methods of caring for and educating young children routinely expected by high-income families may shock and repel low-income families—and vice versa. Routines considered desirable by one group may be seen as inane by another. Guidance strategies believed in some cultural settings to be essential to healthy growth may be considered inhumane and destructive in others. What some consider to be essential experiences for effective early learning, others consider utter nonsense.

Social workers, early educators, and child care professionals have often felt the tension among these opposing views and have sometimes been snagged unknowingly by their own culturally biased assumptions. Effective social policy and appropriate intervention into cycles of poverty and educational failure require understanding of and sensitivity to cultural values and beliefs. The following chapters are intended to shed light on cultural belief systems by describing and analyzing the day-to-day interactions among infants, toddlers, and adult caregivers in socially and economically contrasted day care settings.

Although informal day care arrangements have been a fact of life for generations in low-income families, proprietary and publicly funded day care centers have been used increasingly by working-class parents over the past two decades. Only recently have dramatically increasing numbers of professional, managerial, and clerical level families begun placing their young children in day care centers. Today, child care in licensed proprietary centers is becoming more and more attractive to families of relatively affluent means.

Twenty-five years ago, economic opportunities limited career choices available to women. Social mores dictated that women of middle and upper-middle income stay home to care for young children while their husbands provided financial support. Those who could afford in-house care for their children hired maids or nannies to assist in the care of young children.

Since domestic work was one of the few employment avenues open to working-class women, a pool of cheap labor was readily available. Today, steps to equalize job opportunities for women have decreased the number of those interested in low-paying domestic jobs, while at the same time luring ever-increasing numbers of women of the middle and upper-middle class into the work force, confronting many families with a new dilemma—how to take advantage of rewarding dual-career opportunities while providing acceptable alternative child care [Kamerman 1983, 1985; Kamerman and Kahn 1981; Waldman 1983]. A growing majority of young children are now in child care, and, by 1990, twice as many mothers of children under six are expected to be employed than in 1970 [Children's Defense Fund 1986]. According to Weiser:

> The traditional family, in which the husband worked out of the home and the wife stayed in the home with the children, is part of the historical past and now describes less than a tenth of the families with young children. [1982: 35]

For those mothers who are new consumers of day care, the big question looming on the horizon is, "Can I go back to work without hurting my baby in some way?" For these parents, "hurting" transcends basic physical care and safety. It broadens to include the constellation of experiences that prepare a child to gain access to desirable cultural and financial resources—social prestige and a rewarding career [Lamb 1978].

Folk wisdom and a growing body of research on early socialization processes [Adlam 1977; Anyon 1983; Bernstein 1975; Berlak and Berlak 1981] hold that environmental factors, particularly those encountered in early childhood [King 1978; Florio 1978], may facilitate or hinder a child's later progress in school and in other social institutions that give one access to material resources in this society. King [1978: 148-149] states: "The analysis of the existing system of infant education cannot ignore its relation to the social and economic structure...."

In the past few years, popular magazines such as *Time* and *Newsweek* have featured cover stories on infant care and infant learning. Experts and pseudoexperts abound, offering a rainbow of advice and warning to working parents; few educational researchers, however, have addressed the mushrooming questions now being raised regarding the implications of infant/toddler day care for the socialization of infants and toddlers.

The scattered pieces of infant/toddler day care research give one little clear information about early group care except that there is an increased rate of upper-respiratory infection and diarrhea in group-care babies [Clarke-Stewart 1978], and that quality day care does not appear to disrupt the attachment between mothers and their infants [Kagan et al. 1978; Portnoy and Simmons 1978; Ragozin 1980]. We know little about the dynamics involved in early socialization outside the home. We also know little about the impact of early infant group care on social development and societal class functions. And almost nothing is known about the day-to-day experience of day care as it is perceived by infants and toddlers and the adults who care for them in groups [Belsky and Steinberg 1978].

In the infant development literature, many of those who hold solid research credentials seem to have espoused pro- or anti-infant group care positions based on personal bias rather than empirical evidence, and it is obvious that their views do not encompass all of the possibilities in our contemporary social system. Burton White and colleauges [White et al. 1973, 1978], in infant learning research, has steadfastly disapproved of day care for infants and toddlers:

But assuming the most common situation of a loving, reasonably well-put-together family...it is my considered opinion that attending just about any day care installation full time, is unlikely to be as beneficial to the child's early educational development as his own home during these first three years. [White 1975: 253–254]

Several researchers have been interviewed by journalists writing for popular magazines. This literature becomes significant because of its impact on public perceptions. Psychologist Lee Salk, an outspoken critic of day care, was quoted by Stein [1984] as saying that the children in day care are "walking time bombs" and that parents who cannot take time off from work to provide home care simply should not have children. T. Berry Brazelton, popular author, Associate Professor of Pediatrics at Harvard Medical School, and chief of the Child Development Unit at Children's Hospital in Boston, is one of the professionals who endorse infant/toddler day care. His description of acceptable day care, however, is well beyond that managed by most centers. In a recent interview for a popular magazine, Brazelton is quoted as saying:

One worker for every four children is the absolute minimum, and ideally it should be a one-to-three ratio. The workers should be well trained and should not be competitive with the parents in a relationship with the child. [Minsky 1984: 156]

Brazelton notes that this kind of day care is probably only available to affluent individuals, and that a great deal is expected from child care workers, who are among the lowest paid of all personnel in the field of education.

It is clear that ambiguity and uncertainty exist in both the academic and popular literature concerning day care for infants and toddlers. Before progress can be made in evaluating the impact of the early day care experience on the social structure, some of the fog must be cleared away that is now blurring the essential shape, substance, and texture of infant/toddler day care. The question of early day care must first be defined before it can be judged. Although there are questions about socialization at all age levels, the most pressing concern is focused on the most vulnerable of all consumers of proprietary educational services—the child from birth to three years of age—whose future access to economic security and political power may depend on skills, habits, and attitudes established early in life [Willis 1981; Apple 1982; Giroux 1981].

II

BACKGROUND

Philosophical and Ideological Issues

If the tides of educational ideology could be parted like the waters of the Red Sea, one might find on one side theorists from the Platonic tradition—the innatists, nativists, or maturationists—those who believe that all learning emerges from within. These educators and philosophers believe that human beings are born to be whatever they become; the human infant in this conception is like the rosebud, naturally unfolding into a preordained blossom. Well into the 1920s and 1930s, Arnold Gesell [1928], a researcher at Yale, maintained that environment had very little to do with developmental outcomes, that children's own genetic and biological characteristics determined their intelligence and personality. Obviously, this type of perception has had broad implications for parents and educators concerned with infant care. If infant experiences are inconsequential to one's later development, then adults need only be concerned with providing safe, custodial care in the earliest years. This view implies that growth and learning proceed according to internal rules and personal choices, regardless of environmental circumstances.

The opposite point of view, however, incorporates the seventeenth-century tradition of John Locke [1699], which viewed the newborn's mind as a *tabula rasa* or empty slate. These theorists, the behaviorists, positivists, and empiricists, believe that human learning comes from outside the learner; the environment accounts for most all that a person becomes. Watson [1930], Skinner [1953], and others have established a body of knowledge that bolsters the idea that human beings are really products of their environments. People become scholars or cat-burglars, not because of their genetic makeup or by choice, but because their environment has conditioned them to behave as they do. Subscription to this view also has powerful implications for parents and educators. It implies that human beings can be molded or shaped by the controlling of environmental experiences. This view also shifts emphasis away from a focus on human will and predisposition.

These two bookends of psychological contention have been profoundly influenced by a growing body of research compiled in the past three decades. The work of Piaget [1952, 1962, 1970]; Chomsky [1965]; Kohlberg [1966]; Hunt [1976]; Bloom [1973]; Kagan [1962, 1971, 1978]; and White [1975, 1978, 1979] has made untenable the belief that environmental factors are inconsequential to human development, but they nonetheless support the impact of individual readiness, cognitive style, and reciprocity in learning. A new stream of thought has gained empirical credibility that is neither a maturationist nor a behaviorist view of learning. Piaget [1952], for example, has termed himself a constructionist or interactionist. He has asserted that infants are born with predisposition for certain kinds of thought and behavior, but that they must create their own knowledge through stages of interaction with the environment. Similarly, White [1975], has said that newborn children come into the world with an internal structure that sets an upper limit to their potential, but that the internal structure is not a guarantee of any development or learning. The child is programmed to learn, but without stimuli from the environment no learning can take place. This way of thinking about young children creates pressure on parents to find, and day care providers to produce, ideal infant experiences so that optimum stimuli can be given. Lorenz [1937], Hess [1972], von Frisch [1974], and Lamb [1978, 1981] have done ethological work refining the idea of sensitive periods for learning in which environmental stimuli can have a maximum impact on a child's learning. Hunt [1976] expressed the notion that a match must be created between a child's level of readiness and the exact level of difficulty or discrepancy inherent in a specific learning situation in order for learning to take place.

White has further seized the attention of educated, upper-middle class career mothers by stating:

> To begin to look at a child's educational development when he is two years of age is...much too late, particularly in the area of social skills and attitudes. [1975: 4]

These incisive words from White's popular book have struck a chord of guilt and anxiety in dual-career parents of the middle and upper-middle classes. It seems likely that while they have joined lower-class and lower-middle-class mothers as consumers of day care, they have made new and qualitatively different demands on day care providers.

Historical Context

Child care practices have been strikingly different over time for various social classes. Many traditions from past years would seem strange, even cruel, to modern parents. For example, swaddling, the snug wrapping of infants in strips of cloth or blankets, is an ancient custom that has persisted for centuries in many parts of the world. Although snugly wrapping newborns is considered an acceptable, even positive tradition in most modern cultures, this tight binding of old continued until the child was old enough to walk. Locke described the customary child care in his day:

> ...rolled and swathed, ten or a dozen times round; then blanket upon blanket, mantle upon that; its little neck pinned down to one posture; its head more than it frequently needs, triple-crowned like a young page, with covering upon covering; its legs and arms as if to prevent that kindly stretching which we rather ought to promote...the former bundled up, the latter pinned down; and how the poor thing lies on the nurse's lap, a miserable little pinioned captive. [1699: 103]

The use of such descriptors as "it" and "thing" in reference to young children gives a subtle indication of the perceptions held concerning the humanness of babies. In western Europe during the first half of the eighteenth century, an affluent mother usually sent her newborn infant to the care of a hired wet nurse, who was expected to breast-feed and care for the child, sometimes at the expense of the life of her own infant. Infant mortality rates reportedly reached as high as 80% as wet-nurse mothers, to assure their livelihood, sent their own infants to poorly maintained foundling homes [Weiser 1982].

The writings of Rousseau toward the end of the eighteenth century both influenced and reflected a change in the cultural perception of childhood. He insisted that "everything is good as it comes from the hands of the Author of Nature" [Rousseau 1893: 1]. He argued that rather than an evil creature who must have sin beaten out of him, the young child was born good and innocent. The socialization process tainted the child rather than provided him salvation from original sin. Rousseau's prescription for infant care included breast-feeding by the biological mother, fresh air, loose clothing, and a minimum of interference from adults.

Certain tribes of Native Americans in the 1900s particularly valued physical toughness in their children. To build up the child's resistance, newborns were plunged into water several times regardless of the weather. Their version of swaddling was to securely fasten the baby onto a cradle board that could be conveniently hung inside the lodge, from a tree branch, from a saddlebow, or wherever family members were clustered. Babies were not released from the confines of cradleboards until they were able to walk [Weiser 1982]. American mothers of European descent sent their infants and toddlers to the neighborhood widow or dame for their day care. In these dame schools, a baby might nap on a quilt in a corner of the kitchen while older children practiced reading from the New Testament [Weiser 1982]. Farm and slave children were valued as a source of free labor. Babies barely able to walk were assigned chores.

In the twentieth century, ideas about children have been influenced by two world wars, periods of economic depression and prosperity, and by an emerging academic interest in child development research. At the end of World War II, Maria Montessori wrote such books as *Peace and Education* [1971] and *Reconstruction in Education* [1968] to express her view that the hope for world peace lay in a new education for young children [1963]. She wrote:

> Certainly we cannot achieve it [peace] by attempting to unite all these people who are so different, but it can be achieved if we begin with the child. When the child is born he has no special language, he has no special religion, he has not any national or racial prejudice. It is men [sic] who have acquired all these things. [1968: 6]

In the late 1940s and into the 1950s researchers began to unlock some of the mysteries of infant learning. The common belief that experiences of the first years of life were inconsequential to later development was pushed aside by more complex theories about the development of intelligence and personality that placed greater emphasis on early experiences [Bowlby 1969; Harlow and Zimmerman 1959; Dennis 1973; Erikson 1950; Piaget 1952, 1962; Skinner 1957; Wolff 1963]. In the 1960s, research into infant capabilities flourished and an estimated 23 million books on child-rearing were sold in five years [Clarke-Stewart 1978]. Clearly, the ideologies of early learning as they are implemented in day care centers are deserving of closer examination.

Cultural perceptions of desirable and appropriate care for

infants reflect the perceptions of reality at a given time and place in history. The socialization of a new generation reflects the goals and philosophical precepts of the parent generation within specific social and economic settings. In summary, culture plays a key role in defining acceptable methods of child care.

III

CURRENT THEORETICAL FRAMEWORK AND RELATED LITERATURE

The preparation of children for citizenship in a democracy has long been a stated purpose of education in this country. A continuing debate over inequality, however, has been the focal point of political conflict in the areas of class, race, and gender. Clearly, social and economic strata not only exist but are relatively consistent from generation to generation. Collins [1971] wrote that the basic activity of schools was to teach specific class cultures. He believed that class positions were reproduced by the school's subtle inculcation of "vocabulary and inflection, styles of dress, aesthetic tastes, values and manners." As Marxists, Bowles and Gintis [Bowles 1971; Bowles and Gintis 1972] draw from the work of Kohn [1969] in blaming social inequality on school socialization processes that produce a self-directed middle class and a conforming working class.

Bowles and Gintis focus on what they refer to as internalized norms that provide children from varying school settings with differing values and personality traits that prepare them for respective work positions in the hierarchical class structure and consequently reproduce the social system of inequality. This "correspondence" view has been criticized by Apple [1980] and others as being overly deterministic and not accounting for contradictory structures and ideologies or for normal patterns of accommodation and

resistance on the part of students. Generally, however, all reproduction theorists argue that societies that are economically, politically, and socially stratified produce, through one mechanism or
another, educational structures that reproduce similar stratification [Bowles and Gintis 1976; Willis 1981; Apple 1982; Giroux 1981;
Bourdieu and Passeron 1977].

This study revolves around the assumption that enculturation
involves both the absorption of the individual into the cultural
milieu and the reproduction of the social order. This is perceived to
be a complex dialectical process in which the child is changed by the
socializing group, but the socializing group is also changed by the
inclusion of the child. Social structures at the macrolevel influence
minute social interactions on the microlevel, but the accumulation
of individual social interactions at the microlevel may also eventually have an impact on the structure as individual members accommodate to or resist enculturation.

Bernstein [1979] claims that socialization within the family
proceeds within a critical set of interrelated contexts—regulational,
instructional, imaginative, and interpersonal, as in the following
elaboration:

> Regulation contexts are authority relationships in which
> the child is made aware of the rules of the moral order
> and their various backings. Discipline or behavior
> management serves the important role of socializing the
> child while also, in many families, serving as the focal
> point for child-directed language and thus for linguistic
> code internalization by the child.

> In the instructional context, the child learns about the
> objective nature of objects and persons, and acquires
> skills of various kinds. It is within this context that
> parents and caregivers answer questions, give explana-
> tions, and otherwise share information with the child
> formally or informally to teach concepts or increase
> understanding and awareness.

> In the imaginative or innovating contexts, children are
> encouraged to experiment and re-create their world on
> their own terms, and in their own way. Caregivers
> create this context by allowing children to arrange blocks,
> manipulate art materials, play house, explore their
> immediate environment, and so forth. Language,
> through linguistic code, may serve to encourage, define,
> control, or restrict these activities.

In the interpersonal context, the child is made aware of affective states, his or her own, and others. Caregivers may create this context through their openness to discuss the child's feelings and by mirroring the child's apparent emotional state, for example, "You seem a little sad today." Caregivers may also verbalize their own feelings and the apparent feelings of others, for example, "Sammy feels angry when you hit him," or, "I like it when you remember to close the door."

Bernstein [1979] suggests that the relevant components of a culture or subculture are made real in children through the linguistic realizations of these four contexts within the family, and it might be added, child care settings outside the home. Within each of these contexts, in distinct ways, children may be socialized to restricted or elaborated linguistic codes and systems of meanings and role relationships. All children with normal language development must necessarily have access to restricted codes and the condensed meanings that are obvious and need no elaboration among kin. All children may not have equal access to elaborated codes, however, since there is selective access to the role relations system that stimulates its use, and different levels of family and community support for its use. For infants and toddlers, the early caregivers' role in the broader social setting serves as a model through which the child's exposure to linguistic and role expectations is filtered.

Bernstein claims that social class is unquestionably the most formative influence on the process of socialization. The class structure influences work and educational roles and creates special relationships within families. Further, social class marks the distribution of knowledge within society and has given differential access to the sense that the world is permeable. "It has sealed off communities from each other and has ranked these communities on a scale of individuous [sic] worth" [Bernstein 1979: 477].

Bernstein's sociolinguistic approach to socialization proposes that the patterns of social class are passed on to children, not by the genetic code of their parents, but by culturally induced linguistic codes. Linguistic codes are the verbal expression of one's perceived social role and one's perception of the realities of surrounding social constructs. For Bernstein, linguistic codes bring about social reproduction through the subtle but important implications of the role-relations systems underlying linguistic codes. He outlines two fundamental types of linguistic or sociolinguistic codes—restricted and elaborated. The latter is distinguished by several features:

It is difficult to predict which speech alternatives will be selected or how they will be organized.

Meanings are relatively explicit or context independent.

More time is required for the speaker to plan his or her utterances.

Articulated symbols and rationality are relied upon for a linguistic basis.

Conversely, in his restricted code:

The choices of speech alternatives are more predictable and there is syntactic rigidity.

Meanings are implicit or context dependent.

There is a decreased need for planning time in advance of utterances.

Condensed symbols and metaphors are relied upon for a linguistic basis.

Bernstein further theorizes that a context-dependent (restricted) code or a context-independent (elaborated) code in language use is closely tied to a general context-dependent or context-independent perception of speech. In the restricted code, one assumes that one's listener recognizes and understands the context of utterances. In the elaborated code, that shared understanding of context is not automatically assumed. As Bernstein has refined and adjusted his socialization theory, he has shown [1973] a more complex realization of critical socializing situations in which restricted and elaborated codes can vary in the strength and manner in which they sensitize children toward social meanings and roles.

Of particular interest to the present study is Bernstein's conception of position-oriented and person-oriented strategies for socialization [1971]. Various aspects of the nature of social relations contribute to differing perspectives on the relationships between groups and individuals within a community. Where social relations are such that they support closely shared identifications, shared expectations, and common assumptions, the group is emphasized over the individual. In these settings, position may be used as a basis for social control. In social settings that emphasize the rights and needs of the individual over those of the group, person-oriented strategies are more likely to be employed. Adults tend to give individual (personal) reasons for rules such as, "You might cut your finger if you touch the knife," as opposed to authoritative (positional) reasons, "Stop it because I said so," which are based on the authority inherent in the adult's position. Bernstein has defined position-oriented child care:

> In such a family there would be a clear separation of roles. There would be formally defined areas of decision making and judgments accorded to members...the child develops either within the unambiguous roles within his family or within the clearly structured roles of his age-mate society or both. [1971: 153–155]

In a setting evidencing positional social relations, it is likely that formal titles have an important role in communicating hierarchical relationships among adults and children. "Yes sir, Mr. Jones," would convey recognition of John Jones' positional authority. In contrast, "Okay, John," would convey a more egalitarian or personal perception of one's social relationship with him.

Bernstein's work rotates around the differential educability of children from various social groups depending on whether their use of sociolinguistic code and their perception of appropriate social relations match or conflict with those encountered in the school system. He maintains that schools operate from an elaborated code, at least in part because they are dominated by class fractions that have come to stress such speech codes and attendant role relations. Language-based failure in schools, according to Bernstein, is not a matter of inability in learning or memorizing linguistic nuances, but a deeper problem in which the child's learned social role may make it difficult for him to function if he is placed in a context, such as a school, that requires comprehension and expression in an elaborated code: "...if you cannot manage the role, you can't produce the appropriate speech" [Bernstein 1979: 479]. This may occur because one's own perception of meaning causes one to misperceive role requirements or to perceive them correctly but to see the requirements as nonsensical.

If children are socialized, through the home or the day care center, to emphasize a linguistic code usage that is very different from the linguistic code usage that is traditionally the core of a school setting—they may be thrust into a situation that presupposes role relationships and systems of meanings that are foreign to them. Cook-Gumperz has asserted that a parent's strategy for behavior control "will have an influence on the child's measured verbal I.Q." [Cook 1973: 210-211]. Control strategies tend to be a focal point for adult-child language and thus a key agent for socializing children to either a restricted or an elaborated linguistic code. Additionally, measured verbal I.Q. tends to be weighted toward the use of an elaborated code.

Thus, the minutiae of idiosyncratic adult behavior may be influenced by the adult's socioeconomic status, but may also affect the perceived educability of the child and consequently his or her ultimate access to power and resources in the larger society. The most intimate of cultural phenomena may both contribute to and result from socioeconomic strata.

Bernstein's study of the basic processes of communication and consequential regulative functions has become part of a broadening interest in the behavioral sciences [Fishman 1960, 1965; Cicourel 1964; Garfinkel 1967; Hymes 1962, 1964, 1971; Brandis and Henderson 1970]. The Sociological Research Unit at the University of London has served as a focal point for the exploratory study of familial socialization and linguistic orientation. Henderson [1970] has suggested that middle-class children have access to a greater range of educationally relevant knowledge and are relatively more oriented to principles that relate to persons and objects. This socialization gives them sensitivity to a metalanguage that is critically relevant to their ability to profit from traditional educational experiences. Hawkins [1973] found that working-class children use significantly more exophoric (or context-dependent references) than middle-class children, who showed a tendency toward redundancy in the anaphoric (context-independent) description to the interviewer of a picture or experience shared by both interviewer and interviewee. Adlam [1977], in her further study of exophoric and anaphoric description, has documented class differences in children's perceptual, cognitive, and social interpretation of the interview setting used to collect data. This difference in interpretation of the relevant meanings involved in the sociolinguistic interaction accounts for the various responses of children from different social class backgrounds.

The work of Turner and Pickvance [1973] suggests that an orientation toward the use of expressions of uncertainty is more strongly related to social class than to verbal ability. This I-don't-know phenomenon is seen mainly as a middle-class expression that may result from socialization to flexible thinking within a wide range of alternatives. Turner [1973] argues for further research into the speech of parents as well as their children within critical contexts. Halliday [1973] has drawn upon the work of Malinowski [1962] in his claim that the simplistic language of the very young child can make clear the complex linguistic structures of human beings. He studied the beginning language of a 19-month-old child to trace the particular social functions of various structural elements available to and selected by the child. He states that the internal organization of language is not merely an accident, but rather embodies the social functions that language has evolved to serve in the life of human social relations.

Cook-Gumperz [1979] studied the intersections of specific social contexts and particular strategies or modes of control within Bernstein's restricted and elaborated codes. She uncovered social-class differences in the presentation of social rules to children by their mothers. She argued that class differences are transmitted to children through class-related parental perceptions of control relations. She further provided an extensive description of linguistic behaviors that are theorized to cause differences in the socialization of children across social classes. Class differences deeply affect an individual's perception of work and educational roles [Bernstein 1979], so a dialectical circle is formed in which perceptions of meaning, and hence linguistic code, cannot be realistically altered without altering a given socioeconomic context as well. Socialization in a restricted code may reproduce one's social and economic status, but use of an elaborated code in a subcultural grouping that depends on conformity and group cohesion for survival may be nonfunctional in an immediate sense.

Turner [1973] parallels the work of Halliday [1973] and the Bernstein-Cook model of control [Bernstein 1972; Cook 1973] in proposing that utterances may rely on the context of a social setting for various meanings to be understood. Turner's work confirms the findings of Cook [1973] that linguistic choice is weakly related to modes of control but more strongly related to social status. Additionally, Turner found that social class differences of children seemed to be maintained over time. Working-class children chose linguistic options in an imperative mode that expressed implicit meaning. Middle-class children were found to prefer a positional mode that expressed explicit meaning.

Robinson and Rackstraw [1971] studied the answers of middle- and working-class mothers to the questions of their five-year-old children. These mothers reported how they would answer hypothetical questions. The answers of middle-class mothers contained fewer filler words, fewer irrelevant or sociocentric sequences, fewer appeals to the simple regularity of events, and fewer questions repeated in answer to the child's question. Middle-class mothers tended to give answers that were more complex, included more analogies, and relied more on cause and consequence relationships—responses that may give middle-class children a useful advantage in comprehending their social world. Two years later, Robinson [1973] extended the earlier research by studying the answering styles of children from the earlier study who were now seven years old. They obtained similar and additional results. The maternal style, strategy, information, and mode documented earlier could be used to predict aspects of linguistic and contextual expertise in the children. This further strengthened the fundamental premise of Bernstein's theoretical model.

Although Bernstein [1979] focused on the inherent use of the elaborated code in the school setting, he proposes that middle-class children tend to have access to both codes while working-class children may have access only to the restricted code. To focus attention on the importance of the social or contextual interpretation of language within the school, Florio [1985] cites an anecdote from her field notes in which a young child misinterprets a verbal cue. Florio uses this example of naivete as a foundation for her belief that children must accommodate to the contextual meanings of words, gestures, movements, and actions in order to make sense of both the usual school situations and novel ones. However, Florio does not explore the ramifications of the use of elaborated and restricted codes by teachers and children in her data analysis to see if there may be some instances of school settings in which working-class children may have an advantage over middle-class children in coping with and succeeding in school tasks and social roles.

Ann and Harold Berlak [1981] have developed a set of 16 dilemmas that provide a way of inquiring how teachers, through their schooling acts, transmit knowledge to children along with ways of knowing and learning. They see these dilemmas as a means of representing the diverse, seemingly contradictory patterns that are a part of schooling. According to the Berlaks [1981: 133]: "Dilemmas do not represent static ideas waiting at bay in the mind, but an unceasing interaction of internal and external forces...." The process of society transforming itself is seen as dialectical wherein the individual, although limited and conditioned by the social environment, has the power to create social conditions.

Apple [1982], drawing from previous work by sociologist Pierre Bourdieu, also looks at schooling to understand social reproduction through what he calls cultural capital. He theorizes that the content of one's enculturation may be used, as financial capital is used, to gain access to the power and resources of the dominant culture. He expresses regret that theorists lack the tools to adequately analyze cultural, political, and economic meanings and practices of various groups within modern societies:

> This is especially unfortunate in education since here the everyday meanings and practices constitute the warp and woof of reproduction, contradiction, and contestation in important ways. [Bourdieu and Passeron 1970: 2]

In a society purporting to offer equal access to resources, based largely on merit, there must be further information available concerning the early development of those skills and characteristics deemed meritorious or of socialization styles that result in the acquisition of cultural capital, as well as the mechanisms that allow merit and cultural capital to function as currency in the social structure.

To study cultural transmission further, one must consider the impact of a number of complex social issues. Apple [1982] describes the complexity of cultural transmission by noting the impact of hegemony, the overwhelming presence of a cultural perspective that surrounds an individual and filters his or her cultural experiences. Apple defines this presence as more complex and intricate than manipulation or indoctrination. The body of practices and expectations that surround the child and bring about his or her socialization are not necessarily accepted by the child with passivity.

Malmstad et al. [1983] and Anyon [1981, 1983] have identified and studied the processes of socialization and education. Anyon [1981] distinguishes between passive and active forms of resistance. She also notes the contradictory nature of school knowledge and the realities of modern social structures. Anyon examines the intersections of gender and class for the accommodation and resistance of girls to sex-role ideologies and concludes:

> The analysis above suggests that most girls are not passive victims of sex-role stereotypes and expectations, but are active participants in their own development. Indeed, one could do an analysis of minority girls, and of boys of all races and social classes, to assess how the children react to the contradictions and pressures that confront them. I would argue that accommodation and resistance will be an integral part of the overall processes that all children use to construct their social identities. [1983: 33]

One might infer from Anyon's work that accommodation and resistance are a likely part of the socialization process that goes on between adults and very young children in day care centers as children negotiate their willingness to conform to caregiver expectations, but also as caregivers negotiate their own acceptance or resistance of various ideologies of early curriculum strategies, behavior control, and teacher roles.

Reinharz [1979: 374] has defined the process of socialization as "not merely the transfer from one group to another in a static social structure, but the active creation of a new identity through a personal definition of the situation." In this view, as the children being socialized strive to resolve the psychological and practical conflicts encountered in their role change, they actually create an innovation for the socializing institution. Thus the macrolevel of culture is partly shaped by the microlevel tug-of-war between individual accommodation and resistance and the enculturation process.

The literature indicates that there are general and generative sociolinguistic rules that regulate an individual's talk and his or her ability to negotiate various social relationships; therefore, the acquisition of different codes will result in differential social behavior. This phenomenon, in Bernstein's theoretical perspective, helps account for the reproduction over generations of distinct social class stratification. The concepts of hegemony, accommodation, and resistance also become interwoven in the socialization process.

IV

THE PRESENT STUDY

Purpose

Since there is sufficient information available to predict the relative use of linguistic codes by parents of different socioeconomic backgrounds, it should be of help to ascertain the extent and nature of linguistic code differences and role relationship differences among various day care settings. In addition, the dialectical theory of social reproduction could be enhanced by further information about the give-and-take of early socialization.

It seems plausible that caregivers, in day care centers involving different social classes, may unwittingly participate in the reproduction of unequal social relationships through differential socialization processes. Early socialization may bring about a kind of intellectual and social patterning that sets the stage for one's later perception of meaning and expectations concerning the appropriateness of various social roles. It is also possible that even very young children may selectively resist or accommodate to the pressures of socialization initiated by adults.

Because information concerning the processes of infant/toddler socialization outside the home is limited and little is available that studies this process in terms of linguistic code usage and accommodation and resistance, this study is intended to break ground in an area that may provide functional guidance for those planning and/or regulating day care programs. It may especially be of help to theorists, planners, or policy makers whose goals are focused on progressive school change. It is hoped that this study will shed light on the legacy of socioeconomic status that is passed from one generation to the next.

Bernstein [1971, 1974] in England, and Bourdieu and Passeron [1970] in France have developed new theoretical strategies for relating the problem of educability to various forms of socially controlled cultural transmission. Studies of Black English at the primary and secondary levels have been helpful in clarifying the relationship between socioeconomic level and school success. Since infants and toddlers are in a very formative stage for language development and since day care workers may have an important role in socializing children to differential language usage, a study of infant/toddler day care that examines linguistic code may be helpful in understanding the origins of predictable variations in school success related to social class. This study has attempted to build on the essential theoretical framework of Bernstein's socialization theory while acknowledging the twin pitfalls—seeing all lower-class children as so many pathological deficit systems and seeing socialization differences through the rose-colored glasses of sentimental egalitarianism.

Research Questions

Although Bernstein describes the sources of cultural transmission agents as family, peer group, formal schooling, and work, the introduction to this paper lays a groundwork for including day care as an early source of socialization for contemporary children. Infant/toddler care is an important form of early schooling, although it tends to be viewed as a somewhat nonpedagogical area in the field of education. Literature previously cited indicates the plasticity of very young children and the potential impact of the early environment on social development and learning.

As more and more children are receiving a substantial portion of their early socialization outside the home in proprietary and government-funded day care centers, it seems urgent to examine infant/toddler day care centers at different economic levels to understand more fully the nature of that socialization and the implication of that socialization for reproducing or conflicting with existing class structures.

The study examines certain aspects of verbal and nonverbal interaction between adult caregivers and very young children in day care. It traces the contours of day-to-day events in day care centers as adults from high, middle, and low socioeconomic settings mold a new generation and as the new generation accepts and rejects the molding. The following are major questions that have been addressed:

What is the nature of early socialization as it takes place in day care centers serving families of different social classes?

How is the day-to-day experience of day care negotiated by day care providers, children, and parents?

What are the implications for social reproduction of this early socialization process?

Methodology

Qualitative rather than quantitative methods were chosen for this study since its purpose has been to break ground in a relatively new area of study. Qualitative methodology, because it builds inductively toward the creation of hypotheses, lays a groundwork that can be used later for the quantitative testing of specific propositions. Although qualitative researchers know that any attempt to examine or measure a phenomenon may in some way change it, they believe that in certain behavioral settings, qualitative methodology causes less distortion than traditional quantitative methods. The phenomenological perspective holds that the most important reality in the study of social behaviors is that of the subjective perception of phenomena: "We live in our imaginations, settings more symbolic than concrete" [Bogdan and Biklen 1982: 32]. This approach emphasizes a new sensitivity and creates a pressure on researchers to suspend even seemingly valid assumptions that might interfere with an understanding of social phenomena.

The design of this study is based on the assumption that ethnography can add to the present knowledge of early socialization processes. C. Wright Mills eloquently argued for a holistic integration of the microcosmic and macrocosmic levels in sociological analysis:

Much that has passed for 'science' is now felt to be dubious philosophy; much that is held to be 'real science' is often felt to provide only confused fragments of the realities among which men [sic] live. [1959: 16]

Comprehensive works like that of Durkheim [1938] have today been replaced almost exclusively by tightly limited studies in the tradition of abstracted numerical empiricism. Mills [1959] argues that statistical rigor can never substitute for theoretical imagination. Even researchers with unimpeachable empirical credentials [Clark 1962] have begun to question the proliferation of highly technical but theoretical studies of socialization, schooling, and stratification. Small-scale, arithmetic studies seem to accumulate while broader questions go unexplored. Karabel and Halsey state:

> Caution rather than curiosity is the order of the day, and expressions of intellectual initiative are dismissed as evidence of a lack of methodological realism. [1979: 75]

Different groups of researchers and various research traditions each embody structural weaknesses and flaws. No methodological strategy can hope to monopolize the pursuit of knowledge and truth; an individual researcher can only hope to attain a match between an area of inquiry and a productive technique for compiling and comprehending data. The plea of Mills and others for the holistic integration of microcosmic and macrocosmic levels and for the initiation of theoretical imagination in research provides a strong argument for an ethnographic study that examines the socialization of very young children in day care centers representing various social and economic levels.

The preceding review of the literature indicates the appropriateness of using linguistic code as a lens through which to view the processes of early socialization. The four critical contexts—regulation, instruction, imagination or innovation, and interpersonal interaction—seem ideal dimensions through which to examine adult/child interactions in the day care center. The work of social reproduction theorists also gives credence to a study of early socialization processes geared to provide a better understanding of a social system that shows remarkable consistency of socioeconomic strata over generations in spite of apparent governmental commitment to the goal of equal opportunity in schooling and jobs.

In this research, multicase studies of four day care centers were carried out qualitatively through the use of participant observations, in-depth interviews, tape recordings, and photographs of specific types of events. Field notes served as the primary medium for data analysis.

Since very little work has been done on infant socialization outside the home, this study is necessarily tentative, and as is appropriate in ethnographic research, findings do not serve to test finite hypotheses, but rather serve to create new propositions or hypotheses that could be subjected to examination in future studies. Data gathered in this study have some limitations to generalizability due to the small number of subject populations available for sampling. It is expected, however, that the day care centers selected display to an extent the various types of activities and social interactions available to infants and toddlers in centers serving different socioeconomic levels. It is hoped that this inquiry has produced data that are relevant rather than strictly representative.

Three infant/toddler day care centers were chosen for study from Layfayette and Lee counties, Mississippi and Harris County, Texas. Infant/toddler day care was defined as year-round, full-day institutional care for children, aged birth to three years. Although the allowed starting age varied from center to center, each allowed infants at least as young as nine months. The three centers were selected in terms of their reputations for quality and to provide a random sample stratified with respect to the social class positions of the majority of families whose children attended. Social class position was broadly defined in terms of the occupations of the parents using each center and the amount of tuition charged by the centers.

A fourth center was included in the investigation during the final stages of data analysis in this study because several puzzling and unanswered questions necessitated the addition. Although the fourth center, located in Harris County, Texas, was not studied in depth, as the other three were, the information gleaned from it was sufficient to clarify certain conclusions. The fourth center, which had served as the site for a pilot study, served an executive/elite social class population.

The centers were selected with the aid of three child care experts. The first, from a small town, was a black college professor of child development, public school board member, and former Headstart administrator. She was asked for her recommendations of infant/toddler day care centers that she and her community considered to be of especially high quality but that also were inexpensive enough to be accessible to low-income families. After discussion of the types of families using various centers and the quality of the centers, she suggested five for consideration.

The second expert, from a medium-sized city, was a white educational director for a private foundation involved in developing model educational and family support programs who was formerly a child care director herself. She identified seven possible centers. The third expert, from a large city, was the owner and administrator of a prestigious preschool, director of a preschool teacher training program, and national president of a major child education organization. She was able to list many centers of generally good quality that were used primarily by mixed, middle- to high-income families but stated that there were no infant/toddler day care centers in her area serving a distinctly upper-income clientele. She contended that affluent families were so prone to use in-home care (nannies or housekeepers) that one would only be likely to find exclusively affluent child care center clienteles as a recent phenomenon in major cities. She did recommend several major metropolitan areas having such facilities.

Calls to the first two experts and several hours of calling centers from the telephone directory tended to confirm the assertion that the use of infant/toddler day care centers by affluent families was a trend not seen yet to a large extent in most towns and cities. Eventually three expensive centers serving affluent families were selected from a large metropolitan area. In all, 33 centers were discussed with the experts, but only 15 were listed for further consideration.

I drove to each of the 15 centers that I had not previously visited, and looked at the physical facilities of each, the surrounding neighborhoods, and the appearance of the persons entering and leaving the centers. Generally, the appearances fit the descriptions I had been given by the expert advisers. I then randomly chose one center from each level of high, middle, and low socioeconomic clienteles.

Next, I called the three centers selected and made appointments with the directors. In the first visit to a center identified as lower income, I found that the actual occupations of the parents listed by the director were more mixed than was desirable for the purposes of this study. Another center was selected randomly from the lower income cell. It proved to be a small, all black, privately owned center that advertised taking children from earliest infancy but in fact had recently discontinued taking children until they were "walking and at least starting to get off of the bottle," or about nine months of age.

Participant observation in the three main centers was carried out during approximately 40 hours at each of the three main centers and approximately 10 hours at the fourth center. Initial short visits with center directors were scheduled to explain the study, to confirm tuition costs, to specify parent occupations, to obtain signed permission sheets, and to meet staff members.

Initial participant observations were carried out unobtrusively at various times during the morning, midday, and afternoon segments of the regularly scheduled day. Efforts were made to build trust and to accumulate the first data in a somewhat nondirective way, including the collection of documents giving information about the center's stated philosophy, objectives, and practices. Gradually more attempts were made to initiate informal semistructured, open-ended interviews with adults such as caregivers, administrators, and parents during shift changes (when events of the day were shared by coworkers), lunch and break times, and end-of-the-day straightening times. Additionally, 30-minute segments of activity were audiotaped at various times during observations. On the last day of observation in each center, photographs were taken of routine activities as an additional source of data. Recorded pictures and sounds were used to focus on minute details of the interactive setting and thus to enrich observational records.

Toward the end of the first series of observations in each center, interviews were conducted with directors and key caregivers in a more structured manner. Each was asked a specific set of questions, and each of the interviews was taped and transcribed. The questions were derived from a set used by Cook-Gumperz [Cook 1973] to elicit information about preferred strategies for behavioral control, and adapted to reflect both regional idiomatic expression and the differences in typical behaviors of infants and toddlers from the behaviors of the five-year-olds Cook-Gumperz studied. The purpose of the structured questions was not to attempt replication of a study of control strategies, but rather to provide a point of reference for the relative use of restricted and elaborated codes by caregivers in the three centers.

Analysis of the data compiled in this study was carried out on three levels. First, an ongoing field analysis was implemented to provide for a constant funneling effect. The broad, exploratory nature of the first observations and interviews was examined to bring about a tightening of the research focus. As findings were accumulated, they were subjected to the scrutiny of systematic searches for positive and negative examples that confirmed or negated emerging concepts. The method of starting with data collection and proceeding through field analysis and final analysis to build hypotheses and finally to develop theory has been called formal grounded theory [Glaser and Strauss 1967].

The second phase of data analysis pulled the sweeping nature of this study into tighter focus. A limited number of specific domains were selected for deeper observation and analysis, but with a concurrent effort to continue scanning the overall research settings to maintain a holistic context or perspective. Spradley's Developmental Research Sequence [1979] was incorporated to break down the primary organizing domain—socialization—into relevant taxonomies. This analysis served as a search for the parts of the cultural settings studied, a search for the relationships among the parts discovered, and the development of a set of propositions to explain their relationship to the whole of the culture.

Third, the end of the study, preliminary findings were presented to a group of scholars and lay people who were experts in child development, day care, black studies, and/or cultural studies. Many also had firsthand experience as parents of infants and toddlers in day care in the region of Mississippi where two of the main centers studied were located. The group included seven university professors (five black, one white, one Asian), three in child development and four in multicultural studies. The group also included a regional Headstart director, the head of a housing authority, three day care center directors, and two students (all of whom were black). In an informal roundtable discussion of the findings, the field researcher asked if the group members perceived these features to be typical, and if so, what they perceived the features to mean. The discussion was long (nearly four hours) and animated. The feedback from this discussion was critical in pulling the final analysis into focus.

The most important result of the process of reaching a focus was the late inclusion of a fourth center for study. Several members of the group had referred to the developmental or child-centered model for child care as "an import from the white community." Their rejection of an approach to child care seen in the primarily white centers as not relevant to the black community fit findings from the first three day care centers studied, but called into question a virtually all-white, affluent center that had been visited during initial screening but had not been selected for in-depth study. There appeared to be striking parallels between the teaching styles embraced by this affluent center and the all black low-income center. Data from the fourth center were added to the study and made a part of the final analysis.

To simplify this report and make it more readable, letters were arbitrarily assigned to each of the centers and fictitious names were assigned incorporating those letter designations. For example, center A is called Alphabet Academy and each subject there is given a name starting with the letter "A."

V

THE SETTINGS

To illustrate similarities and differences observed in the centers, three hypothetical days have been synthesized as a composite of items gleaned from field notes and inferred from multiple observations. The following description of typical days is an account of objects, actors, and events that are similar to those actually seen over a much longer period of time. These segments are compressed into a single fictional day to collapse into a manageable format the data from hundreds of pages of field notes, more than two hundred photographs, and nearly 50 half-hour segments of audiotaping. The following three descriptions illustrate the usual flow of events, types of social and verbal interaction among actors, activities, and the environmental settings of each of the centers. During data collection, the three centers were coded A, B, and C; therefore, in order to protect the privacy of the participants in this study and to simplify this report for the reader, pseudonyms beginning with those letters have been assigned to each of the centers and persons described below.

Alphabet Academy

Just before six o'clock in the morning, Arla Mae Aiken pulls into the deeply rutted gravel driveway between a small self-serve gas station and the school and parks her car for the day. It is cold and dark as she unlocks the front door of the tiny frame building and chats with a man in khaki overalls and worn work boots who is holding a 15-month-old girl on his hip. After Mrs. Aiken turns on the lights, two wall heaters, and a small free-standing electric heater (with a piece of wire mesh propped across it), she takes a small handful of cash from the man. The child stands quietly and watches as the two adults discuss the possibility of snow and Mrs. Aiken counts the $28 in bills and coins and writes a receipt. Mrs. Aiken locks the door after the man leaves and turns her attention to the little girl who is still standing in the middle of the classroom. The girl has both arms tightly clasped around a satchel stuffed with disposable diapers, a few articles of clothing, and a baby bottle of milk.

Mrs. Aiken takes the bag, and as she unbuttons the child's jacket, she says, "Addie, why your daddy bring you bottles?" She laughs and gives the child a brisk hug and pat. "You don't need no bottles do you." She then pushes the child's possessions into a high cabinet and carries the bottle to a refrigerator in a small side room. She tells Addie to "go on and play now" then proceeds to lock and unlock the front door and greet other parents and children from one to five years of age. A cold gust of air fills the room each time the door is opened. Many of the parents stand outside the door when it is unlocked and after watching their children enter, simply say, "Bye," "You be good, now," or "Hey, gimme some sugar 'fore I go." Other parents come into the classroom and visit for a few minutes. Some say, "Good morning, children," and receive an instant chorus of, "Good morning, Miz..." Several focus their conversation on the teacher and discuss such things as relatives who are ill, church activities, the price of children's clothing in a nearby resale shop, and concern about impending layoffs in a local factory.

By seven-thirty, the classroom vibrates with the noise and activity of a dozen toddlers and preschoolers. Plastic cars with the wheels broken off, crooked toy pots and pans, and other well-worn toys are taken from a built-in wooden toy box in the corner of the room that is so large that even the oldest children must stretch, head first, deep into the box to reach toys on the bottom. The youngest children must rely on toys abandoned by older children. A group of the older boys and girls make a train by sitting on a variety of carlike toys, each child tightly hugging the waist of the child in front of him. Since none of the cars have wheels, loud grating, scraping sounds rhythmically fill the room as the children push and scoot in unison. Several toddlers stare as the older children squeal and shriek with delight. Occasionally Mrs. Aiken admonishes them, "Hold it down. Y'all are gettin' entirely too loud. Ainetta, I'm gonna make you get in the corner." Mrs. Aiken sits down on a wooden barrel with a board across the top and begins reading the story of Peter Rabbit to two two-year-olds and one one-year-old who press close, leaning against her knees.

A three-year-old girl, Athalene, climbs onto the only shelf in the room to reach a picture book of nursery rhymes. She quietly mutters, "I love dis book, I love dis book," as she pulls a chair off a table and sits down. As she turns the pages of the book, she chants the words to nursery rhymes that fit each picture. Several children who hear her begin chanting with her. Two girls pull chairs close to her and join in her activity. Athalene begins, "Pease porridge hot..." Her two playmates yell, "Huh uh! No it ain't, that's 'Wee Willie Winkie'!" They argue animatedly. "Wee Willie Winkie" wins, so Athalene pulls the book away and walks across the room. The two playmates run after Athalene and take the book away from her.

Athalene's howls rise above the noise in the room. Mrs. Aiken turns to Athalene, "Hey, what's wrong with you?" Athalene stifles her crying to respond, "They took my book."

The two playmates with the nursery rhyme book quickly contend that Athalene "wasn't sharing." Mrs. Aiken sends Athalene to stand in the corner. Athalene presses her face against the corner of the room with her arms hanging limp by her sides. She turns her head slightly and casts a sullen look at her two former playmates who have run back to their chairs to continue chanting nursery rhymes. They yell, "Mrs. Aiken, Athalene is lookin'." After about five minutes, Athalene has slumped onto the floor in the corner and is watching the activities around her. She gets up, glances at the teacher, who is busy wiping a one-year-old's nose, climbs back on the shelf, and stretches for the remains of the book section. She finds a Bible and several coverless segments of picture books. She collects a new set of playmates, including a two-year-old girl, and retreats to a wall at the back of the classroom. They sit close together, backs to the wall, feet outstretched, and holding the Bible and book segments out with the dignity and formality of official choir books, sing an almost recognizable version of an old Baptist hymn about the cleansing blood of Jesus. Mrs. Aiken notices them and walks to Athalene, taking the Bible, "You know you don't play with the Bible. Why you so bad today? You gonna act right?"

By eight o'clock, Mrs. Aiken has started preparations for the academic portion of the day. She sends two and three-year-olds to use the toilet and begins to check the diapers of the youngest children. She rearranges several articles on a small Formica and chrome dinette table that is a visual focal point in the room. Above it a large decorative calendar shows every child's name and birthdate. The table serves the varied functions of bookkeeping table, teacher's desk, and receptacle holder for first aid, medicine, lost-and-found, money, office supplies, and candy-and-gum type contraband brought by the children. It now becomes the diapering table. Mrs. Aiken lifts a 15-month-old boy, Arthur, onto the table and lays him on his back. She pulls his blue jeans and torn plastic pants off. He is wearing a thin, frayed cloth diaper pinned with large safety pins. Mrs. Aiken removes the soggy diaper and leaves the room with it. Arthur lies very still, looking up at the ceiling. Slowly and carefully he feels the edge of the table with his right hand and then holds the chrome edge as he stretches slightly to look out the door Mrs. Aiken has exited. She returns with a fresh disposable diaper and proceeds to dress him. When she is finished with his new diaper, she stands him on the table and pulls his jeans up. He grins at her and she smiles and says, "Gimme some sugar." Arthur leans forward and they kiss. Mrs. Aiken gives Arthur a playful swing to the floor and a firm but loving pat on the rear.

Mrs. Aiken turns her attention to the older children and coaches them to get the room cleaned, "Come on now, get this stuff cleaned up. It's time for devotional." When a four-year-old boy whines, "Do we have to?," Mrs. Aiken turns to him and says, "Adam, you know good and well we have devotional every day at eight. Get them cars put up and sit down. No, you ain't sittin' by Ainetta—all you two wanta do is talk."

As the last toys are hurriedly slammed into the toy box, the children gather around two low tables made from eight-foot by four-foot sheets of plywood painted red and blue. Mrs. Aiken supervises the 19 children as they arrange the child-sized wooden chairs in a rigid pattern around the tables. All chairs face forward— chairs at the backs of the tables are pushed under, chairs on the sides of the tables are placed, one in front of the other, along each side, and chairs in front are placed with the chair backs touching the tables. The children over three years of age sit around one table and those under three sit around the other. Some are told exactly where to sit by the teacher. Athalene, who is three, takes a seat with the younger children. Mrs. Aiken chides her, "Those little babies don't want you sittin' with them." Mrs. Aiken turns to Annie, the two-year-old sitting beside Athalene and says, "You don't want her sittin' with you, do you?" Annie grins and shakes her head. "See, they don't want you over here. Git over there with the big kids and sit down. Okay, everybody, shut your mouths and open your ears."

Mrs. Aiken walks to the center of the room facing all of the children. She stands beside her barrel and board stool, which an older girl has positioned properly for her. "Okay, kids, place your right hand over your heart and face the flag. Let's say the pledge." Children stand in front of their chairs and begin the chant in unison. All of the older children have their right hands over their hearts.

Almost every one-year-old has both hands holding chest or abdomen and stands silently watching the teacher and older children.

Everyone sits. The one-year-olds climb into their chairs and sit with feet sticking out straight. Mrs. Aiken says, "All right, children, let's sing our morning song. They sing in a strong, melodious voice, "I wash my hands every morning, ah hah! I wash my hands, do you?" While most of the one and two-year-olds join in the hand-washing motions, only the older two-year-olds attempt the words to the song. Most of the children seem very familiar with the next song. They sing, "Be careful little hands what you do, for the Father up above is looking down on us below, so be careful little hands what you do." At the end of the songs, Mrs. Aiken announces, "Now we gonna say our nursery rhymes. We gonna start with Adam today." Adam stands to Mrs. Aiken's right and begins, "One, two, buckle my shoe." The one-year-olds follow a few of the hand and body motions of the nursery rhymes as each child takes his or her turn to lead.

When the sixth child is coming to the front of the room to take her turn, there is a loud knock on the door. Mrs. Aiken opens the door for Miss Ames and her daughter Audrey. Mrs. Aiken goes back to her barrel stool as Audrey, a 17-month-old, drags a cloth diaper bag into the room. Miss Ames, who is a 19-year-old student, leans in the doorway and tells Mrs. Aiken, "I taken Audrey to the doctor this mornin'. You shoulda seen that chile. Ohwee! She pitched the biggest fit you ever seen. You never seen such hollerin'." They laugh and Mrs. Aiken turns to Audrey, "What you holler for, Audrey?" Miss Ames turns to leave, then says, "I put her in pants today but I know she wet." She looks back at Audrey with a look of mock disgust, "Bye. Bye. You ain't gonna say bye to me? You mad? Bye." She leaves.

Mrs. Aiken puts away Audrey's jacket and diaper bag. While Mrs. Aiken's attention is diverted, the children begin to laugh and talk. Ainetta, who is sitting behind Athalene, puts her feet on the rungs of Athalene's chair and pulls on the chair back until Athalene is balanced precariously on the back two legs of her chair. Athalene scrambles to get her balance, grasping at the table and the sides of her chair, but Ainetta keeps her chair pulled back. Athalene appears very uncomfortable but not overly concerned. Mrs. Aiken loudly instructs all of the children to get quiet. "Y'all hush. Don't make me lose my temper. Athalene and Ainetta, I ain't gonna tell you no more. Ainetta, you change places with Anthony. Git over there. I told you. Now settle down." Mrs. Aiken escorts Audrey into the bathroom to use the small plastic potty. When she returns to the classroom, Audrey follows her, wearing only a blouse and shoes.

Athalene points at Audrey and shouts, "Miz Aiken, look, she ain't got no pants on!" As Mrs. Aiken attends to Audrey, she sternly scans the table of older children and announces, "I can hear you from the bathroom and I know every one of your voices." The room is silent for a few seconds, then Ainetta accuses Anthony of having looked at Audrey without pants on. Anthony protests that it's okay to look at little babies. Ainetta flips her shoulder toward him and replies, "Well, you shore cain't look at me."

The one and two-year-olds fidget and squirm in their chairs but make no attempt to get up. They poke and kick at each other playfully. The youngest boy yawns and rubs his face with his fists. He vigorously rubs his nose with the back of his hand then looks down and sees that his hand is slick with mucous. He stares, points to it for a long time, looks around, then finally turns around in is chair and with a dazed expression, sucks on the knob of the chair. A two-year-old girl beside him goes to the dinette table and painstakingly tears a piece of tissue from a roll of toilet paper. She returns and firmly holding Arthur's head with one hand, wipes his runny nose. He grimaces but does not resist. Mrs. Aiken returns, directs Audrey to a chair, and resumes the nursery rhyme activity.

When Anthony, five years old, is called to the front, he pouts and hangs his head as he mumbles the words "Bah, bah, black sheep...." The chanting group quickly takes control of the rhyme and shouts the words in perfect unison. While most of the older children attend to the group activity, the one- and two-year-olds begin to rub their eyes and faces, roll their heads, and swing their legs and feet.

When Ada, a one-year-old, is given her turn, she stands silently with a startled expression. Several older girls yell out suggested rhymes to her. Mrs. Aiken tells them, "Hush, Ada know what she wanta say." Finally, Ada holds out her hands and clicks her tongue. Mrs. Aiken announces that Ada wants to say "Hickory, Dickory, Dock." She helps Ada say, "Hickory, dickory." By the word "dock," group momentum again takes control of the rhyme and several girls giggle as they shout the words.

Mrs. Aiken says, "Stand up, we gonna sing 'The Wheels on the Bus.'" There is a quick scraping of chairs as the children hurry to their feet. The teacher stands, arms outstretched, as she leads the song. The children gleefully rub their eyes and pretend to pout as they sing, "The babies on the bus say, 'wah! wah! wah!' all through the town." They can hardly wait for the next line. They dance and wag their fingers as they shout, "The mommas on the bus say, 'Hush yo mouth! Hush yo mouth!' all through the town." Their next song is, "I'm bringing home a baby bumblebee." The children giggle as they sing, "Won't my momma be surprised of me, I'm mashing up the baby bumblebee, now there's blood all over me." They squeal and laugh as they rub their hands on each other and sing, "I'm wiping off the blood of the bumblebee."

Mrs. Aiken says, "Okay kids, that's enough, it's time for exercises." Instantly, the children run to the open area of the classroom. She directs them, "Line up. Move over Ainetta, don't get in front of the little babies. Ready? Twenty jumping jacks. One, two, three, move those arms, five, six...." The small frame building shakes to the rhythm. Several of the one-year-olds become very animated and laugh as they jump and shake in crude imitation of the calisthenics. The two oldest two-year-olds look very serious and follow many of the prescribed movements fairly accurately. Just past eight-thirty, the children have finished their twists, bends, leg lifts, and arm rolls. Mrs. Aiken tells them to get ready for snack.

The older children fidget and tussle in line, waiting for their turn to wash their hands or "use it" in the small bathroom that has one toilet, three plastic potties stacked in a corner, and a huge sink hanging at a precariously lopsided angle. While several girls are inside, an older boy annoys them by pushing open the door, which has no latch. Mrs. Aiken gets the one- and two-year-olds into their chairs and pushed under the table while older children quickly pass out cups, paper towels, and small piles of crackers to each place setting. At the "big kid's" table, a flurry of discussions and arguments begin about the crackers. As Mrs. Aiken wipes each "little baby's" hands with a damp, soapy paper towel, the older children put snacks in front of them and then carefully push the snack items just out of each small child's reach. Arthur holds out his hand toward the crackers and looks at Anthony, who has just placed them there. Anthony pushes the crackers a little farther away. Arthur thrusts his hand toward the crackers and says, "Uh." Anthony puts his face close to Arthur's face and firmly repeats back a very firm "uh!" Arthur puts his hands in his lap and looks away. When all of the children are served and seated, Mrs. Aiken says, "Put your hands together. Okay." The children recite together, "God is great, God is good, let us thank Him for this food, Amen." Mrs. Aiken pushes the youngest children's snacks within their reach, then pours juice, cuts and peels pieces of apples for the children, and continues her verbal directives, "Sit up, you're gonna waste your juice. Quit talkin' now and eat—please. Anthony! Quit messin' with people. Anthony, go get in the corner."

Mrs. Aiken answers a knock on the door just after nine. Some of the children who have finished snack run to greet the woman, Mrs. Anderson, who walks in holding hands with an 18-month-old boy. Mrs. Anderson, the director and "big kid's" teacher, tells Mrs. Aiken, "Good morning. Everything goin' okay? I had to stop and pick up Andy. His mama's car broke down." Then to the children, she says, "You all get your snack cleaned up. It's time for class. Ainetta, did you study your numbers last night?" Ainetta answers, "Yes, Ma'am," but gets into an argument with Adam who asserts that "you lyin'." Children hurriedly clear the tables. Annie starts to cry loudly because one of the children has whisked away her crackers before she has finished." Mrs. Anderson says, "Adam, you don't take people's food while they're still eatin'."

Andy, the one-year-old who has just arrived, is escorted to the side room and given a snack by Mrs. Anderson while Mrs. Aiken wipes tables and puts away snack supplies. All of the children except Anthony have been instructed to sit on the floor by the wall. Anthony brings an adult-sized mop into the room and mops vigorously at a juice spill. The children sitting on the floor are involved in intense and animated interactions. Two older boys negotiate with a four-year-old girl and she agrees to sit on one's lap. Several discuss a TV show they have seen, "Did you see that white girl and that white boy that was on...?" A three-year-old girl pulls a one-year-old girl into her lap. Mrs. Aiken sees her and says, "Okay, if she bites you or somethin' you're gonna be in trouble."

Mrs. Anderson returns and announces that it is time for class, "Okay, big kids get your chairs and let's go." Carrying or dragging chairs, they crowd into the tiny side room facing a back door that leads to another small frame building. Through the noise and commotion there is the piercing sound of Audrey wailing. Mrs. Aiken steps into the small crowded room and asks the older children what has happened. Mrs. Anderson laughs and says that Audrey tried to "steal" one of Andy's crackers and the "big kids punish her." Mrs. Aiken laughs and looking at Audrey repeats, "Ohee, the big kids punish Audrey." Audrey's crying (four distinct howls) ends immediately and she walks back to the empty class-room and climbs onto a chair.

It is almost nine-thirty and the room is quiet for the first time since six. Mrs. Aiken directs the one and two-year-olds to the table where Audrey is sitting and untying her shoelaces. Mrs. Aiken yanks her foot up onto the table and briskly ties her shoelace while she says, "Let's settle down now and get ready for class." Arlin, a 35-month old boy, the oldest child in the "little babies" class, watches Mrs. Aiken closely. He has been coming to the Alphabet Academy since he was four weeks old. It has been a year since the center stopped accepting very young infants. The staff decided that the youngest infants required too much individual attention so now children are accepted only "when they are able to stand up and walk enough to get out of the way of the big kids, and when they are starting to get off the bottle," since no bottles or pacifiers are given to the children. Mrs. Aiken pushes Arlin's chair under the table. He holds on to the sides of his chair and looks up at her. She smiles and says, "Arlin, you bad?" He grins and shakes his head vigorously, "Uh, uh." She laughs, "Yes you are, you bad."

Mrs. Aiken walks toward the huge shelf and cabinet structure that provides the only storage in the room besides the toy box and table tops. Arlin points to two posters high on the top shelf. He says, "Cass [class] high inna kie [sky]?" As Mrs. Aiken steps on a chair to reach the posters she answers, "No, it ain't in the sky, it's on the shelf." Two of the youngest girls pound on the table and playfully kick at each other under the table as Mrs. Aiken tapes the two posters onto the wall under a row of handpainted capital letters. One poster has large numerals from 1 to 20 drawn in rows of four and separated by a tic-tac-toe type grid. The other has nine circles of faded construction paper glued on it in a random pattern.

Mrs. Aiken stands formally in front of her seven young students and says, "Arlin, you be first today." Arlin hops off his chair and hurries to the front. With his nose almost touching the painted letters, and putting his index finger carefully on each letter, he monotones slowly, almost without letting his lips move, "Ay, beh, ce, dah, ea, eh, jhe...." When he points to L and says "euh," Mrs. Aiken corrects, "Huh, uh, that ain't right, do that one again. No, it ain't eyem. That's ayell. That's right, good, good." When he reaches Z, Mrs. Aiken says, "Why Arlin, you jus' about know your alphabets. You'll be goin' to the big kids class soon. You done real good." After he tediously plods through his numbers and colors with occasional prompting, Mrs. Aiken sends him back to his chair and says , "Now, Annie it's your turn. Ada, you and Audrey pay attention now and quit foolin' around. I'm gonna have to separate you."

Mrs. Aiken stands with her arms folded and watches as Annie says the alphabet more quickly than Arlin. Halfway through the letters she begins to glance over her shoulder at the other children and fumbles and loses her place. Mrs. Aiken expresses her annoyance and insists, "You not even tryin', Annie, you know these." Annie only makes it through the first three numerals before she has to have prompting with each number. Mrs. Aiken snaps, "Annie, pay attention, five, no, five, no, that's the four."

As the younger children take their turns, Mrs. Aiken holds their right hands and slowly monotones the correct response for them as they touch each letter, number, and color. The only requirement she makes of even the youngest is that they keep looking at the items as she helps them point. Ada never takes her eyes off the appropriate items throughout the recitation. Audrey, however, is constantly reminded, "Audrey, look here! Audrey! Look up here."

The recitations are completed before ten-thirty, and most of the children appear to be restless and fidgety. The youngest boy looks as if he were in an hypnotic trance. Mrs. Aiken passes out paper and pencils to the children—plain white paper to all except Arlin and Annie. They get ditto sheets with uppercase and lowercase letters faintly visible in dotted lines. They both begin outlining the letters as they talk, "I gah [got] bee [big] peince [pencil]." "Aauh, my peince mo [more] bee." Mrs. Aiken interrupts them, "Annie, get over here by Ada. All you two wants to do is talk." Annie moves by Ada and points to Arthur, "Loo [look]." Mrs. Aiken quickly moves to Arthur, who is asleep face down on his piece of paper. She gently pulls him from his chair, washes his face in the bathroom and walks him around the room until he appears to be alert. She says, "Arthur, you musta stayed up too late last night. Come on now, don't go to sleep no more."

Mrs. Aiken tells the children with plain paper to draw houses on their paper. She bends down and draws a house and says, "This is my house. Andy, I believe you live in a circle house." The children stay seated in their chairs while Mrs. Aiken takes the papers and staples them onto the wall. She then looks through a stack of Walt Disney books, each of which contains a single record. She says, "Hmm, let's see, should we listen to Davy Crockett or The Black Hole?" Arlin looks up and says "Ba [black] ho [hole]?" Mrs. Aiken answers, "You wanna listen to The Black Hole? Okay, we'll listen to Black Hole and Mary Poppins." She pulls her barrel and board stool in front of the children and plugs in a small plastic record player. For over 30 minutes, the one- and two-year-olds sit while hollow, squawking voices from the toy record player tell tales of British chimney sweeps, nannies that fly, and space ships that are endangered by a black hole in the depths of the universe. Mrs. Aiken holds up the book and turns pages whenever the record gives a chiming sound. The children again become dazed. A few revive briefly as Mary Poppins sings "A spoon full of honey makes the medicine go down, the medicine go down...." But, before the spaceship is finally rescued, Arthur, Annie, Ada, and Andy are asleep in their chairs. Audrey fidgets, picks at her nose, and pulls her shoes off again. Mrs. Aiken firmly says, "Audrey, cut that out. You a bad lady today. You a bad lady! Look up here. Look at this book."

Just after eleven, Mrs. Aiken stands and says, "Okay, go sit on the floor by the wall, we'll play ball until the big kids come back." She begins putting the records and books away as the children rouse and leave the table. Arthur walks around the back of the table but realizes that his way is blocked by the electric cord stretched from the record player to the wall outlet. He stops, looks at the cord, and turns to look at Mrs. Aiken. He points to the plug and says, "uhh." She doesn't notice him. He reaches for the plug, stops, looks at Mrs. Aiken again, then after several seconds, he finally crawls under the cord and walks toward the other children.

The seven one- and two-year-olds are sitting on the floor with their backs against the wall. Mrs. Aiken says, "Arthur brought a ball today. You wanna play ball? Arthur, since you brought it, you can be first. Stand over there, no get back, stand back over there. Here stand here. Annie, you be quiet or you cain't play. Hold out your hands, no both hands, no, you can't catch it like that. Put your hands together, not that way, like this." The children squirm as they watch and wait for their turns. Only Arlin and Annie seem to know what Mrs. Aiken expects of them in this game. Nevertheless, they all seem eager for their turns.

A few minutes before twelve, the back door crashes open and the "big kids" troupe in, dragging chairs. They shove the chairs under their table and line up to wash hands for lunch. The sounds of the youngest children are lost in the noise, talking, and laughter of the older children. As before, the older children stand in line waiting to use the bathroom while the younger children sit at the table and wait for a teacher to wipe their hands.

Miss Ames, Audrey's mother, comes in the back door carrying containers of food. She is the school's cook and part-time assistant teacher. She has prepared lunch in another small building but Audrey has not seen her since their arrival at school earlier in the morning. Although Audrey is seated about 20 feet from her mother, she begins to cry as soon as her mother comes into view. Tears run down her cheeks as she screams. Mrs. Aiken and Mrs. Anderson are both in the side room helping Miss Ames put servings of food onto plates. They are directing older children who serve as runners, carrying plates from the side room to the two big tables in the classroom where children are sitting, waiting to be served.

Audrey's cries become louder. She ignores requests from Mrs. Aiken to "hush." Annie, who is sitting beside Audrey, tries to get Audrey's attention. She gently shakes Audrey and says, "Huh [hush]!" Audrey screams. Annie pounds the table in front of Audrey and puts her face close to Audrey's. Without ever taking her eyes off her mother, Audrey shoves Annie away with one hand then screams even louder. Annie says "huh!" again and gives

Audrey a firm slap. Audrey, who is now sobbing and gasping, grabs Annie's face and digs her fingernails into Annie's cheeks.

Annie begins to howl. Mrs. Anderson sees Annie's cheeks and firmly commands, "Audrey, get in the corner." Audrey springs out of her chair and runs to the corner. Her howls and sobs are muffled since her face is pressed tightly into the corner. Mrs. Aiken tells Mrs. Anderson, "Miss Ames say Annie hit Audrey first." Mrs. Anderson laughs and says, "Oh, all right, Audrey, you can go in there to your mother." Audrey sniffles and rubs her face as she runs into the kitchen to her mother. After the last plate has been served and the blessing has been said, Miss Ames comes into the classroom carrying Audrey and a plate of food. She sits in Audrey's chair and, holding Audrey on her lap, feeds her the lunch. When Audrey tightly closes her lips and turns her head, Miss Ames says, "You better eat 'dis. I'll take you to gramma's. She'll make you eat it." Audrey quickly opens her mouth.

After lunch, the oldest children help with clearing and scraping the dishes, wiping the tables, and arranging frayed plastic nap mats on the floor. After the children have been to the bathroom (or had their diapers changed) they are instructed to lie down and "go to sleep." All of the little ones except Annie are asleep within minutes. Annie twists and turns on her mat, playing with her hair barrettes and her shoelaces and poking at the child who is nearest her. The teachers sit in the side room drinking iced tea and talking about the children and the events of the day. It is one o'clock and Mrs. Aiken's first break since six. She duplicates an activity sheet on the ditto machine to use the following day with her class, then prepares to leave since her workday ends at two.

The children are required to be quiet and still on their mats. All of the children finally fall asleep. At three, several of the children who have awakened are allowed to get up. By three-thirty, the children are up from their naps and preparations are under way for afternoon snack. Even the youngest children seem familiar with the sequence of events and the routines. They immediately sit in their chairs at the tables and hold out their hands for wiping.

After snack, the children are allowed to play until their parents come for them. As in the early morning playtime, they empty the big toy box and cluster into small groups. The boys run around the room pushing toy cars and other objects and making loud sound effects. Many of the older girls look at books and play school. They role-play the morning's routines by chanting nursery rhymes and calling out the letters and numbers painted on the walls. Two five-year-olds compete to see who can say the alphabet backwards most quickly. The girls also herd younger children to the front of the classroom and imitate the teacher by holding the one-year-olds' hands up to touch each letter as the older girls slowly call out the alphabet. As in the morning, the children are animated and active. Toys crash into the toy box and children shout and tussle as they play. Spontaneous chants of the alphabet, numbers, and nursery rhymes quickly spread through the room. The children's play is vibrant and rhythmical. The youngest children tend to be spectators. They follow older children with apparent immunity. Older children who fail to "watch out for the little babies" are quickly sent to stand in a corner. When Mrs. Anderson sees Athalene trying to pull Addie into her lap, she says firmly, "Okay, Athalene, if she bites you or somethin', you're gonna be in trouble!"

The younger children are allowed to assert their rights with each other, however. When Arthur suddenly notices that Annie is holding the ball he brought to school, he chases her several times around the room, then catches her shirt and tackles her. They both crash to the floor. Arthur has Annie pinned down on the floor but she still manages to hold the ball just out of his reach. They tussle and yell. Mrs. Anderson shouts, "Annie, you know that's his ball. Give it back." They stop immediately and Annie begrudgingly gives the ball back.

Arlin's mother arrives at four-thirty. Arlin, who has been crawling under a table, giggling, and chasing another child, looks up and sees his mother. His appearance changes immediately and he begins to cry. As he stands motionless, with tears dripping from his chin, Mrs. Anderson laughs and says, "I tell you he's an adult until you come. He's an adult all day. Now he's a little baby."

By five, all of the children have been taken home and Mrs. Anderson locks the doors.

Balloons and Bunnies Learning Center

At six-thirty in the morning, Betty Ballew drives into the parking lot of the clean and spacious Balloons and Bunnies Learning Center. It is located on a corner that intersects a neighborhood of moderately priced but well-manicured apartment complexes. Across the street is a new shopping strip with a convenience store and laundromat. The center is within walking distance of a shopping mall and a medium-sized medical center.

The center is a modern brick building with the facade of an old-fashioned red schoolhouse on its front, complete with fake bell and bell tower. The fenced playgrounds contain attractive wooden play structures and a small swimming pool that is covered for the winter. Just inside the front door is the director's office area. Her desk and office equipment are positioned in the entry hallway facing the door so that she functions as gatekeeper as well as director. Just past her desk is a door that leads into the main part of the building. The preschool areas form a large, open U-shape around an enclosed nursery room in the center back. Observation windows on both sides of the nursery make it possible for adults standing in the preschool areas to see inside the nursery. The nursery as well as the preschool areas each have safety doors leading directly into small fenced playgrounds. At the front of the building, adjacent to the entry area, are a teachers' coat closet and restroom and a large, modern kitchen. The preschool areas have child-sized sink areas as well as doors labeled girls and boys that lead into two toilet areas. The nursery also has doors leading into the two restrooms as well as a specially designed diapering area with a sink, built-in shelves and cabinets.

As Miss Betty unlocks the front door of the center, two other cars park and she is joined by the center's kindergarten teacher and a woman in a white nurse's uniform. The nurse is carrying a seven-month-old boy and a large denim diaper bag. She says, "Good morning, Miss Betty." All three women exchange pleasantries. Then Miss Betty takes the baby's hand, smiles, and says in a high voice, "Hey, Ben. I like that little sailor suit. You look so cute today." The mother answers, "He'll probably spit carrots all over it and look like a dirt ball before the end of the day. Won't you, huh?" The women laugh as they enter the building. The kindergarten teacher heads to her classroom in the back left portion of the open horseshoe area. Ben's mother and Miss Betty walk back to the nursery. They discuss Ben's morning feeding and his diaper rash as Miss Betty puts three baby bottles of formula into the tiny countertop refrigerator and arranges disposable diapers, extra clothing, and a tube of ointment in a small storage cubbyhole labeled with Ben's name.

The mother hands Miss Betty the baby in exchange for the empty diaper bag. Ben begins to whimper and clings to his mother's clothing as Miss Betty takes him. His mother says, "I'm gonna come back. I'm gonna come back. I hafta go to work now. You be a good boy today." Miss Betty takes Ben's hand and helps him wave goodbye as his mother leaves, "Say bye bye to Mommy. Bye bye, Mommy."

A few minutes after eight, Miss Beth arrives. She rushes in with a big grin and breathlessly bubbles, "I love you Miss Betty, darlin'. Don't be mad at me. I was almost on time but I hit every red light. No kiddin', I'll never do that again." Miss Betty answers, "It's okay, I don't think many of my kids are here yet. Besides, you're just a couple of minutes late. Everybody's had breakfast except Brad and his mom said he'd eaten."

Miss Betty leaves the nursery and claims her two and three-year-olds from the mixed-age group of children who have been cared for by the kindergarten teacher from six-thirty until other staff members begin to arrive at eight. Several children talk at the same time as they walk with Miss Betty to their area, an open arrangement of learning centers with two long, low tables in the center. This area is just outside one of the doors to the nursery. As the children chat with Miss Betty and scatter to play with blocks, dolls, puzzles, and Legos in the learning centers, Miss Beth sticks her head out of the nursery door and asks, "Miss Betty, Brad's fussin', should I give him a cracker or somethin'?" Miss Betty responds that she thinks a cracker would be fine.

Inside the nursery, Miss Beth opens a small container of saltines. She says, "Here Brad, quit fussin'. Do you want this cookie? You're starvin' ain't you." Brad takes two crackers and walks across the carpet, still whining. Several other one-year-old boys hurriedly gather around Miss Beth holding out their hands and grunting for the crackers. Miss Beth looks at one 17-month-old boy who is standing back and watching quietly. She hands him two crackers and the chorus of grunts around her becomes louder and more insistent. One boy beside her starts to whimper so she hands him one cracker. Then she looks at the remaining two boys and says, "You all don't need no cookies. I know you had breakfast." They continue whimpering and reaching so she breaks one cracker in half and gives each boy a piece. Both walk away. One munches happily, the other, Billy, starts to cry. Miss Beth says, "Billy, Billy! Okay, gimme that cookie back." Billy hesitates, looks at his cracker piece then up at Miss Beth. He stops crying and eats his cracker. Miss Beth wraps the remaining crackers and returns them to a shelf beside a large, hand-lettered sign that says, "Miss Beth, DO NOT give babies crackers unless they are sitting down!"

Ben, the seven-month-old boy who is the youngest child in Miss Beth's group of six children, has watched the cracker proceedings silently from an infant bouncer seat. Although the bouncer has wheels so that it can be moved about, Ben sits still, sucking his pacifier and watching the other children. After Miss Beth puts on a clean apron that has the center's name and trademark on the pocket, she turns on a radio and tunes it to a country and western music station. She says, "How 'bout let's listen to some music." She stuffs a handful of tissues into her apron pocket then makes her way from child to child, wiping noses. She holds each child's head with her left hand and firmly wipes the child's nose with her right. The children grimace but tolerate this procedure. She says, "Look at your nose, Billy. I done wiped your nose all day yesterday." She throws all of the used tissues away then picks up toys and books that have been scattered and returns them to a low shelf while Willie Nelson croons softly from the radio. One boy follows her and takes a toy owl with a clock-face body off the shelf. She says, "Uh uh, Billy. Leave those alone—please, darlin'. Uh, uh. Here, Miss Beth is gonna get down some puzzles."

She slaps three simple wooden puzzles down on the floor and dumps puzzle pieces in front of several children. Blaine, an 18-month-old, who is the director's son, begins carefully putting puzzle pieces shaped like farm animals into the proper holes in one puzzle board. Brad picks up a puzzle piece, examines it, then puts it in his mouth. Miss Beth quickly snatches it out and says, "Brad, don't put that in your mouth darlin'. You never know where that thing's been. Here, uh uh, Brad, I'm gonna put it away if you keep tryin' to put it in your mouth. Look, it goes right here. Do like Blaine. No, turn it around, baby. You're no good at puzzles, are you?" She pats his hair and puts the puzzle away on the high shelf. He turns and picks up a piece of Blaine's puzzle. Blaine throws back his head, closes his eyes, and howls. Brad grins, looks at Miss Beth, and grabs more puzzle pieces. She unclamps Brad's fists and takes the puzzle pieces then quickly gathers the rest of the puzzle and gives it back to Blaine. Blaine continues to cry.

Miss Beth gets a covered, tip-proof cup from the refrigerator and gives it to Blaine. He stops crying and drinks the juice. Brad reaches for the cup and Miss Beth says, "All right, you're gettin' in the playpen. I know it's ugly of me but you're just gonna have to stay in there." She whisks him into the pen. Just as she turns around, Billy is climbing onto the rocking chair. She whisks him off the chair and chides, "If you fall and bust your head open, I'm gonna hafta rush you to the hospital." He grins and runs back to the chair. She grabs him around the waist as he tries to climb on it again then says, "Uh, uh, stay off that rockin' chair. You're gonna kill yourself." The third time she grabs him off the chair he squeals with laughter. She looks at him, shakes her head and says, "Billy, you're a little devil, you know it." She laughs as she hoists him over her head. Her expression changes and she says, "Oh, you stink, I better change you."

The nursery is divided into two parts by two large shelf and cubbyhole structures. The back of the room has a large flat carpet with letters, numbers, and designs in bright colors. Along two walls are rows of cribs designed with clear plastic ends so that babies can look out and caregivers can look in. A rocking chair, two playpens, and a low storage shelf covered with toys are the only other pieces of furniture in this area. The third wall has an emergency exit door and two low windows with pictures of animals painted over them. At the front of the room are a diaper-changing sink and countertop, a low table, several high chairs, and, pushed back into the corner behind a playpen, a variety of playhouse furniture items and riding toys. Most of the wall areas are covered with colorful paintings, posters, decals, and pictures. One large poster by the door shows schedules for four children in picture symbols. Stickers that depict bottles, toys, cribs, diapers, and an outdoor scene are stuck on the poster to represent individual schedules. The stickers are neatly colored in crayon, but the schedules seem to be somewhat out of date. The alphabet is painted on one wall just at the edge of the ceiling. Several small mobiles with built-in music boxes are hung from the ceiling over cribs and over the diapering area. An adult of average height can just reach them to wind the music mechanism. Access between the two areas of the room is blocked by a playpen, a desk, and an adult-sized chair that have been pushed between the two shelving structures.

Miss Beth pushes the playpen aside and carries Billy to the diapering area. Brad, who is still in the playpen, whines and tries to get his foot over the side. Miss Beth looks over her shoulder and says, "Brad, if you don't stop cryin' I'm never gonna let you out." He continues to whimper "ou, ou [out, out]." With one hand, Miss Beth rolls out sanitary paper over the diapering countertop. She lays Billy on the paper and changes his diaper. The three one-year-olds who are playing in the carpeted area of the room notice that the playpen has not been pushed back completely, leaving an escape route to the forbidden front end of the nursery. They squeeze through the crack and toddle straight to the riding toys that have been hidden in the corner. Miss Beth calls to them as she tears off the used strip of paper and throws it away with the soiled diaper, "Uh, uh, uh! Don't come in here. You know better." She carries Billy on her hip and herds the escapees back into the carpeted area saying, "Ya'll just fight over that tricycle. Besides, you'll fall off it and bust your lip or somthin'."

She hands toys to Brad in the playpen and to Ben in the bouncer. Then she picks up toys from the floor and gets down two large balls from the high shelf. She tosses one toward Blaine and one toward Billy. Brad cries and holds out his hands toward the balls saying, "Ba, ba [ball, ball]." Miss Beth says, "You don't need no more toys. You've got so many toys in there now you can hardly walk around." Brad watches the other children for a long while, then he rests his head on his arms on the side of the playpen and rolls his head around. He rubs his eyes with his fists and yawns. He whimpers, hangs his head over the side of the pen, bounces up and down a few times, and finally, with a dazed look, begins to pull his eyelashes out.

Miss Beth rushes around the nursery changing diapers, cleaning the room, and responding to squabbles over toys. When Ben begins to cry loudly, he is put in his bed and given a bottle. When Billy touches Blaine's ball and Blaine cries, Billy is banished to a playpen. Brad is taken out of the playpen for a short time but when he bangs on the window glass with a wooden toy he is put back in.

At eleven, Miss Beth gets out a tablet of printed forms that provide information for parents about their child's day. Miss Beth prints each child's name on the top of a sheet. The first line of the form says, "Today I was—happy, busy, curious, fussy." Miss Beth carefully circles the word happy on each form. She fills in times for each child's diapering, feeding, and napping for the day. Then, at the bottom of each sheet, on the lines marked comments, she tediously writes "He was happy and smiling at me all day."

Before noon, Miss Beth has swept the room, put away all the toys, and straightened the sheets and blankets in each crib. She gets a book and picks up each child and places him on his bottom in a semicircle on the floor. Blaine resists and starts to cry so she leaves him and sits on the floor facing the semicircle of one-year-old boys with her back to Blaine. She reads nursery rhymes to the group. Her voice and facial expressions are animated and bright. Blaine crawls over and sits near the others. Most sit frozen and silent where she has placed them. Their eyes are wide as they look and listen. At the end of the short book, Miss Beth puts down the book and sings, "I'm bringing home a baby bumblebee, won't Miss Beth be so proud of me. I'm stomping on the baby bumblebee...I can't remember the rest of the words." Then Miss Beth says, "Let's do ring-around-the-rosies. Stand up and make a circle. Here, Brad and Blaine, hold hands. Billy, hold Brad's hand. No, silly, over here. Hold hands! You all know how to make a circle, you just don't want to."

Miss Beth checks the clock then looks out the door the see if the cook has brought lunch to the older children. She warns the children not to get any toys off the shelf, "Y'all leave those toys alone now. I just got it all cleaned up. Miss Barbara's bringin' your lunch in a minute." Brad will not leave the toys alone so she puts him back in the playpen. Several children are whining and Blaine is crying loudly. Miss Beth sits in the rocking chair with Blaine in her lap as the other children stand around her. Miss Beth looks at Blaine and says, "Please, don't cry, sweet pie, Miss Beth has a headache." Ben wakes up and starts to cry, too. She puts Blaine down on the floor, and just as she lifts Ben out of his crib, Miss Barbara arrives with a tray of food. Blaine and Billy and several others scramble past the playpen barrier and run to the table. Billy climbs on top of the table while Miss Barbara turns her back to lift

Brad out of the playpen. Miss Barbara attempts to guard the food as she positions children in chairs.

Miss Beth changes Ben's diaper, stuffs his soiled diaper and the changing paper into a full trash can, then puts him into a highchair. She gets a jar of carrots from his cubbyhole, opens it, and sits down to feed him from the jar while Miss Barbara struggles to feed the older babies at the table. Blaine clamps his mouth shut and will not permit Miss Barbara to feed him macaroni. She pushes the bowl of macaroni away then tears tiny bits of bread and pushes them in front of him. He picks at the bread and eats most of it between whimpers. Brad sticks his finger into his chocolate pudding and licks it off. Miss Barbara tells him, "Brad, eat nicely. Here, try some of these green beans." Brad squeezes his lips together and turns his head. Miss Barbara laughs, "All right then, you can have 'em dipped in chocolate pudding. That's all right with me." She dredges the green beans in chocolate pudding and reoffers them. Brad gingerly tries a bite then allows Miss Barbara to feed him until the chocolate pudding is gone. By turns, Miss Barbara arranges, mashes, and tears the food on various children's plates. Between her offers of bites to them, most feed themselves with their spoons or fingers. Billy fingerpaints with his chocolate pudding but will not taste any of the food.

Miss Beth and Miss Barbara clear the table, wipe each child's hands with a wash cloth, and then carry the children to cribs. Brad and Billy are put back in playpens and Ben is put back in his bouncer seat and given a pacifier. Most stand in their cribs and cry. Miss Barbara leaves with a tray of dirty dishes as Miss Beth passes out bottles and tries to get the children down for their naps. She turns off the light and the radio, closes curtains over the two windows, and calls out firmly for individual children to "lay down and go to sleep." She stands at the foot of Blaine's bed and jiggles his crib as she sings in an off-key, monotone voice, "And if that billy goat won't pull, papa's gonna buy you a cart and bull...and if that cart and bull gets runned over, papa's gonna buy you a dog named Rover...."

Before one, most of the children are sleeping soundly. Miss Beth has checked each child, straightened blankets, put away empty bottles, and rinsed a pacifier she has found on the floor. She is ready to leave for her one-hour lunch break when the director comes in to relieve her at one. The director, Miss Bonnie, has looked through the observation window to be sure her son, Blaine, is sleeping before she comes into the room. Miss Bonnie asks Miss Beth about Blaine's morning. As Miss Beth collects her purse and sack lunch, she says, "He was just fine. He was happy all the morning, but he didn't eat no lunch, just bread." As she steps out the door, she pauses and says, "I thought that new little bitty baby was s'posed to start today. When's she gonna start?" Miss Bonnie says, "It's a little boy. His name is Brent. Mom said she would have to take him for his shots today but she might bring him in the afternoon." Miss Bonnie sits in the quiet room doing paperwork until Blaine wakes and sees that his mother is in the room.

When Miss Beth returns at two, Miss Bonnie is sitting on the floor with the only two children who are awake, Blaine and Billy. Each boy has a piece of drawing paper and several thick crayons. They sit quietly scribbling on the papers while Miss Bonnie watches and praises their efforts. Miss Beth puts her purse away, laughs and talks with Miss Bonnie for a few minutes, then she throws her arm around Miss Bonnie and with a big grin says, "You'll send Miss Betty in here to help me if that new little bitty baby comes, won't you?" Miss Bonnie answers, "I don't know, Beth, we'll have to see how many big kids we have." When Miss Bonnie says goodbye to Blaine and turns to leave, he scrambles to his feet and begins crying loudly. Miss Bonnie leaves and Miss Beth turns her attention to Blaine saying, "Blaine, I'm not gonna leave you darlin', I wouldn't leave you for anything in the world. Miss Beth is gonna be right here."

All of the children are awake and back on the floor playing by two-thirty (except for Brad, who is back in the playpen). A woman enters the nursery carrying her six-week-old son. She is accompanied by her four-year-old daughter and Miss Barbara, the cook. Miss Beth says, "Oh, she's a real little bitty baby. She's adorable. Ain't she cute, Miss Barbara?" The mother says, "His name is Brent." All three adults lean over the crib where he has been placed as they discuss him. His big sister presses her face through the crib bars. The mother says, "Just feed him his bottle whenever he wants. He'll only take about three ounces and you have to burp him after each ounce. He can have his pacifier, but just don't leave it in his mouth all day. And that's all—well, change his diaper now and again." Miss Beth reviews these instructions and in a worried voice asks how she will know when to feed him. Both the mother and Miss Barbara laugh and assure her that she will know when he's hungry. The mother adds, "Oh, and he has a little bit of a rash so put this ointment on him when you change him." Miss Beth asks where the rash is and the mother answers, "You'll see it. Just put the ointment around his, uh, you know, his, uh, diaper area."

The mother leaves to take her four-year-old daughter to the prekindergarten classroom. Miss Beth says, "I'm gonna change her in her crib." Miss Barbara looks puzzled, "Who?" Miss Beth points,

"Her, that new little bitty baby. I'm scared to pick her up. I'm afraid I might hurt her."

Soon the nursery is filled with Brent's high, thin wail. Miss Beth's hair, which earlier was pulled back into a neat pony tail, is now frayed and hanging in her face. She mutters to herself, "Oh, that little bitty baby is waking up." She hurriedly fills in the parent report form for Brent. She circles the word happy, and writes, "He was happy and smiled at me all the afternoon." After she tries three times to spell the word enjoyed, she erases and adds the line, "I had fun having her." She tapes it on the cubbyhole designated for Brent. She turns just as Billy begins pounding on the transparent end of Brent's crib with a pull toy. Miss Beth yells, "Uh, uh! Billy, don't bother that little baby. You'll get in the playpen."

Miss Beth changes Brent's diaper in his crib then gingerly lifts him out. She has a worried expression as she rocks him gently in her arms. He continues to cry. She says, "I b'lieve you're spoiled you little sweet pie. I can't hold you all day." The one-year-olds fight over a toy so she puts Brent back in his crib and tries to put his pacifier in his mouth. He is crying too hard to hold the pacifier. The door opens and Brent's big sister runs into the room. Her teacher follows her and tells Miss Beth, "I told her she couldn't come in here but she just pitched a little fit. Is it okay if she looks at the baby for a minute?" Miss Beth says okay and the girl stands at Brent's crib, holding his tiny hand through the bars. She softly says, "Hi, baby. Whatsa matter?" as she looks suspiciously around the room. Brent stops crying and turns his head toward his sister. She rubs his hand that is clasped around her finger as she continues talking to him. Miss Beth begins talking to the sister about how tall and pretty she is getting to be and how long her hair is, then she pats her on the head and tells her it is time to go back to her own classroom. Miss Beth says, "He'll be all right, I promise. You go on back to your class now, okay."

The silence is broken as Billy pushes Blaine down and Blaine starts to scream. Ben, again in the bouncer seat, also starts to cry. Miss Beth puts Billy in a playpen, in spite of his loud objection, and hands him and Brad toys from the high shelf. She puts several books on the floor for the other boys and puts a pacifier in Ben's mouth. Then she runs hot water in the diapering sink and stands one of Brent's bottles in the water to warm it. She paces between Brent's bed where he continues crying and the sink where she feels the temperature of the bottle. Finally she goes to the door and signals Miss Betty that she needs her. Miss Betty comes to the door and Miss Beth says, "That new little bitty baby is cryin' and I don't know if I should feed her or not. See if Miss Bonnie will let you come help me for a few minutes before you leave (Miss Betty's work day normally ends at three-thirty).

Miss Bernice arrives to care for Miss Betty's 12 two- and three-year-olds, and Miss Betty comes into the nursery to help with the new baby. Miss Betty picks up Brent and pats him as she asks Miss Beth when he ate last and whether or not he has been changed. Miss Beth passes out saltines to quiet the one-year-olds and puts Ben in his crib with a bottle as she answers Miss Betty, "I already done changed her, but Miss Barbara said she ate at one and wouldn't be hungry 'till four. I'm scared I'll make her sick if I feed her this soon. Do you think I done right?" The one-year-olds munch their crackers and watch the two women. The boys seem unusually subdued and passive. One boy crawls under a crib and sits with his back against the wall as he eats his cracker. Blaine stands beside Brad's playpen and whimpers and looks at Miss Beth when Brad stretches over the side reaching for his cracker.

In the two- and three-year-olds' classroom, Miss Bernice calls out that it is time to put the toys away so the children can "do something fun." The three-year-olds laugh, talk, argue, and play. Only a few attempt to put toys away. Miss Bernice, a retired grandmother who works part-time in the center, tries to put the toys away faster than the two-year-olds can get them out. She says, "I don't believe you all know how to clean up. Hasn't anyone taught you how to put your things away. I have stickers for the ones who clean up the fastest. Who wants a sticker?" Several girls yell, "I'm the fastest! I'm the fastest!" as they cram blocks and toys onto shelves. All of the children are three years old except three two-year-old boys. Bert is almost three. He looks around at the room cleaning as he stands in the playhouse area pretending to wash his hands in the toy sink. Barry and Bernardo are both 24-month-olds. Bernardo is the only black child present in the two- and three-year-olds' class today. He does not attend the center regularly but is a drop-in today because his grandmother is unable to keep him, as she usually does. Barry was graduated to this class a few weeks before his second birthday because Miss Beth could not manage him in the nursery any longer and he was spending most of his time in the playpen.

While Miss Bernice continues to lead the room cleaning, Bernardo wanders off to the prekindergarten class and is escorted back after a few minutes by two older children. Miss Bernice calls to him to help clean. Barry walks to the child-sized sink. He looks for a long time at Miss Bernice, then turns to the sink and slowly feels the faucet and handles. He glances over his shoulder at Miss Bernice then looks all around the sink. Again glancing over his shoulder, he bends down and carefully opens the cabinet doors below the sink. He peeks up over the top of the cabinet door at Miss Bernice, then reaches inside the cabinet for a soap dish and bar of soap. He examines them both carefully and brings the soap to his mouth, carefully tasting it and feeling it. Then he stands up and puts the dish and soap on the counter behind the sink. Suddenly, he hears Miss Bernice coming toward him. He jumps and puts his chubby hands behind his back and grins at her. She silently takes his hand and leads him to an open area where colored numbers are pasted on the floor. She says, "Sit down, Barry, we're going to listen to a story. Come on everybody, let's sit down." She leaves Barry sitting on the floor on a number with several older children while she goes to find Bernardo. As soon as her back is turned, Barry is up and exploring again. He knocks over a small bulletin board that is propped by a wall. He walks over it and stands with his back and arms against the wall surveying the room.

Miss Bernice pulls Bernardo onto her lap and holds him as she sits on a small chair and reads a picture book to the group sitting on the floor around her. Barry continues to move around the area. He has found a tiny metal car and he says, "Rrrrrmmm! Rrrrrmmm!" as he pretends to drive the car along the window sills. He watches Miss Bernice from time to time but ignores her requests to sit down and listen to the story. Bernardo sees Barry's car and struggles to get out of Miss Bernice's lap. She frees him and he joins Barry at the window. The three-year-olds listen and make comments about Miss Bernice's story. Miss Bernice then closes the book and lays it on the floor beside her. She cups her hands and says, "Let's catch a bumblebee." The children sing with her, "I'm bringing home a baby bumblebee, won't my mommy be so proud of me." On the last verse they sing, "I'm squishing up the baby bumblebee, now there's blood all over me. I'm washing off the baby bumblebee, now my mommy won't spank me." Then they sing, "The wheels on the bus go round and round." After the verse that describes the babies crying on the bus, Miss Bernice and most of the children sing, "The mommies on the bus say 'shhhh, shhhh, shhhh!'" However, in spite of Miss Bernice's glare, three children gleefully shout, "Shut your mouth, shut your mouth!"

At the end of the songs, Miss Bernice says, "Okay, everybody sit down at the table real nicely for me and we'll paint some pretty pictures. Come on Bernardo and Barry, sit down for Miss Bernice so you can paint too—please." She moves the children around and seats the girls at one end of the tables and seats the boys at the other end, "No, I want you here. You come sit here." When all of the children are seated, she places sheets of drawing paper in front of the children, gives each a long paint brush, and puts one tiny bottle of paint between every two children. Several older girls complain about the color they are given and Miss Bernice trades several jars of paints until the children seem satisfied. Even Bernardo and Barry begin dipping their brushes and painting on the papers. After about ten minutes, Miss Bernice tells the children, "Put your picture on the science table for me so it can dry. Oh, that's so pretty. Yes, yours is pretty too. I like all that red." Miss Bernice takes Bernardo's and Barry's papers and carries them herself to the science table. She returns just in time to see Bernardo carefully painting the palm of his left hand and Barry about to paint Bernardo's shoulder. She lunges for the two paint brushes and says in a high voice laced with tension, "Come wash your hands, boys. Let's get ready for snack, please."

Miss Bernice escorts Barry and Bernardo to the sink and helps them wash off the paint, then leads Barry into the nursery for Miss Beth to change his diaper. When he returns she firmly instructs him to stay in his chair at the table and wait for snack. It takes Miss Bernice another 15 minutes to get all of the children washed and through the restroom. She allows only one child in the restroom or at the sink at a time. She pulls the younger children's pants down for them before sending them in to use the toilet. One little girl wants to go into the restroom with her friend. She says, "I have to go too." Miss Bernice answers, "You can go when she comes out." The little girl says, "But I have to go!" Miss Bernice says insistently, "You can go when she comes out." The little girl says in a louder, higher voice, "But I want to go now!" Miss Bernice snaps, "Well, you're not going now—you can go when she comes out!"

Barry has been sitting at the table alone. He has twisted, turned, rubbed his face, yawned, and by the time Miss Bernice returns and all of the children are sitting down, he has fallen asleep. Miss Barbara brings cookies and punch and Barry wakes up as he hears Miss Bernice say, "Fold your hands and let's say the blessing." Barry and Bernardo grab their cookies and begin eating before the children have finished saying, "God is great, God is good...." After snack, Miss Bernice takes the children outside on the playground to play until five.

Just before five, Billy's mother comes into the nursery to get him. She sees Billy and laughs, "There's my big boy. Come give me a hug. I missed you today. Did you have a good day?" Billy lays his head on his mother's shoulder and grins. Miss Beth puts her hands on her hips and with a look of mock disgust says, "He's a mama's boy that's what he is. Just a big ole mama's boy." She grins but Billy's mother looks a bit hurt. She says, "He's really pretty good about me leaving him. You're a good boy aren't you." Billy grins at his mother and holds on to her. She smiles, glances at his parent report form, then gathers his belongings and says goodbye to Miss Beth.

Miss Bernice comes into the nursery at five. Her children have joined the older children to wait for their parents to come for them. Miss Beth gives a few instructions to Miss Bernice about the new baby and then says, "I am so tired. I'm gonna go home and do nothin' tonight." Miss Beth says goodbye to all of the children and then leaves for the day. After she is gone Brad's mother arrives. She notices the new baby and says, "Oh, boy, you all have a real baby, baby. Aww, isn't he cute. It makes me want to have another one." Miss Bernice pats the new baby and says, "Yes, I think I'll have to take him home with me."

Color-Coordinated Country Day School

The Infant School

At seven Camille Caldwell unlocks the bolt locks on the front door of a building that is part of Color-Coordinated Country Day School. This campus is designated for infants from three months to 18 months of age. Staff members and parents refer to it as the infant school. The building, originally a graceful two-story brick home, is situated on a corner lot in a neighborhood that is largely owned by investors. The neighborhood is located directly between the sky-scrapers at the city's center and one of the world's largest medical centers. It is within walking distance of three museums, a huge zoo, and several exclusive high-rise hotel and apartment buildings. The neighborhood evolved over several generations from an affluent residential neighborhood to a decaying inner-city ghetto, but is now edging back to its former status as highly valued property. The neighborhood is checkered with extremes—extravagantly redone mansions to crumbling duplexes, professional business offices to seedy bars, new condominiums to charred remains of buildings.

The front door of the infant school has a number-coded lock so that whenever the bolt locks are open, anyone knowing the correct combination can punch the numbered code and enter without knocking. A well-polished red sports car is parked on the street in front of the building. A tall man in his 30s wearing a gray pinstriped suit steps out of the car, gets a diaper bag from the back, then helps his 16-month-old daughter out of her car seat. He opens the front gate and they walk hand-in-hand to the wide front porch. He quickly punches numbers into the door lock, then, still holding the little girl's hand, says, "Careful. That's it. Come along now," as he guides her into the building.

In a dignified British accent, the man says, "Good morning, Camille. Did you have a pleasant weekend?" Camille walks toward him smiling and answers, "Yes, thank you, and you?" Then she takes the girl's hand and, kneeling on the floor, says in a melodious voice, "Good morning, Clarice. Don't you look nice today. Would you like to take your coat off?" Clarice holds out her arm and Camille removes it while the father places diapers, extra clothing, empty baby bottles, and a pacifier in the cubbyhole marked with Clarice's name.

The man squats on the floor with his daughter as she begins to gather toys that are neatly arranged on low shelves in the room. She brings a stuffed dinosaur and a man's hat to him. He takes the stuffed animal and says, "I believe this is a brontosaurus, see, it has a long neck." Clarice takes the toy back and, putting the large hat on her head, turns and walks back to the shelf. The man stands, talks to Camille about his daughter's allergy medication then turns and says, "Well then, Clarice, give Daddy a kiss. Bye, bye." Clarice kisses him but begins to whimper as he leaves. Camille picks her up and says, "Here, come look out the window, then you can wave to your dad." They stand at the front window and Clarice waves her hand as Camille says, "Wave bye, bye. Bye, bye, Daddy." Clarice's father stops at the end of the sidewalk and waves back.

Camille puts Clarice down on the carpeted floor and walks with her through a set of french doors into the area designated for the group of children who are called the explorers, children generally between 12 and 18 months of age. The front area of the infant school is designated for babies from three to 12 months of age (or whenever the staff believes the child is ready to make the transition to the explorers' environment). The area for the youngest infants is a rectangle about 30 feet long and 12 feet wide. It is divided into three parts. At one end is an area that holds seven small cribs, a large rocking chair, and an infant swing. A large, bright mobile hangs just over the rocking chair. Mobiles, music boxes, and manipulative toys are mounted on the rails and sides of each of the cribs. Several cribs have stuffed animals or rag dolls in them.

The center portion of the infant area is larger than the crib section. It contains a diapering area with a mobile attached to the wall that hangs just a foot over a plastic-covered diapering pad. A bright geometric design is affixed to the wall alongside the pad. Cubbyholes for seven infants are within arm's reach for an adult changing a child's diaper here. Premoistened wipes, liquid hand soap, paper towels, and spray bottles of germicide and air freshener are also close by. The cabinet below is closed with a child-proof lock, but a string of bright wooden beads hangs from the knob low enough to be accessible to crawling babies.

On the opposite wall are low cabinets, with the doors removed, that have been adapted to create a play space for babies. Carpeting, a mirror, pictures, and toys are mounted inside. A long countertop over the cabinets holds a microwave oven used to warm bottles and baby food, a row of baskets filled with collections of toys, and a stack of picture books with thick cardboard pages. Above the counter are high storage cabinets and at the end of the cabinet is a refrigerator.

Inside the refrigerator are seven trays, each labeled with a child's name, that hold bottles, baby food, and medicine. Inside the freezer there are several small containers of frozen breast milk that are also labeled. Clipboards hang on the side of the refrigerator with written schedules for each child and a logbook of daily comments written by staff members. A new chart labeled with the correct day and date is taped on the front of the refrigerator. It has a column for each child and spaces so that the children's arrival, departure, feeding, diapering, and sleeping times can be entered along with parent and staff comments. A code is used to designate whether diapers that have been changed are wet or soiled.

Along the bottom edge of the wallspace left open are mounted such things as a mirror and a pegboard. The pegboard is covered with dangling toys that can be manipulated but not removed. On the floor are a padded ramp, a portable plastic bar used to hang toys in reach of a reclining infant seat, an eight-inch-high table and matching chair, and a large beach ball.

The third section of the infant area has two low wooden shelves; a closed fireplace with a row of baskets holding various types of toys on its mantle; and a miniature couch, overstuffed chair, and hassock that are proportioned to the size of the babies. Beside the tiny couch is a small wicker basket of picture books. On the wall, two feet off the floor, is a knobbed plastic coat rack. On it hangs a man's hat, several bright colored vests, unbreakable beaded necklaces, and an eclectic collection of purses. All of the infant area is carpeted in soft beige, and a strip of wallpaper trim circles the room with a row of white geese wearing red ribbons. The three sections of the infant area have nothing to obstruct babies from moving from one end to the other if they are mobile. The french doors leading from this section into the explorers' area make it possible for younger and older children to see each other.

In the explorers' area, there are two rooms separated by patio-type sliding glass doors. The first room has a diapering area that is like that seen in the infant area except that it has a toy dangling from a stout elastic cord over the diapering pad instead of a mobile. On a shelf beside the diapering area are clipboards with a staff logbook and charts. The explorers' chart has less space to report feeding and diapering but more space to report the specific activities of each child. Under the diapering counter is a cabinet space that is carpeted, wallpapered, and mirrored to make a hideaway for the children.

There are high shelves with neatly arranged baskets of toys and low shelves with carefully spaced objects in color-coded boxes, baskets, trays, and canisters—a different color for each shelf. The low shelf has a pegboard cover that fits on its front so that the shelf can be opened or closed. A low climbing structure, a five-foot-long platform with a rail around it, is pushed against one wall. It has a tiny staircase and a wide ramp for climbing on and sliding off. Low wooden stairs make it possible for children to look out a window that has a heavy sheet of clear safety plastic mounted over its bottom half. A padded tunnel the size of a small doghouse has rounded openings at both ends for children to crawl through. A chalkboard is mounted low on the wall with a basket (out of the children's reach) holding thick chalk and a small eraser. Wooden riding toys are parked near the french doors and a pillow and several stuffed animals are tossed invitingly in a corner with a basket of picture books.

A hallway from this room to the kitchen is blocked with a half door. The hallway doubles as a coat closet with labeled coat hooks along one wall. The kitchen has two low tables, each seating four children. Past the kitchen is an office space with a locked door to the upstairs area that is used by staff members as a lounge, a conference area, and a storage space.

Through the glass sliding doors of the explorers' diapering and motor activity room is the doorway to the last room. It is a slightly smaller room that has low shelves around two walls. As in the first room, the shelves are lined with carefully arranged, color-coordinated containers. Several of the shelves have covers for opening and closing them. Tiny tables and chairs are arranged near the shelves. One corner of the room houses sturdy, child-sized play furniture and is equipped with dolls, blankets, dishes, and plastic fruit. A low half-door leads into a small restroom with two little toilets and one sink. The half-door restricts entry by children but allows visual supervision by adults. Another door leads to a covered deck and a fenced playground.

By eight, three of the seven infants under a year who make up the infant group are present. They are cared for in the front area by

Camille, a certified Montessori teacher who is also the director of the infant school, and her assistant, a young woman named Carmelita. A mother and her three-month-old son arrive for the child's first day at the center. The mother has planned to stay all morning since the center requires a primary caregiver (parent, grandparent, or babysitter) to stay with the child for at least most of the first three days. Camille spends 30 minutes showing the mother around the infant area and explaining the scheduling and chart procedures. The mother describes her baby's usual routines as Camille writes on her tablet.

The mother tells Camille, "I want to keep him on the breast as long as I can. I'll still nurse him for his morning, evening, and night feedings, and I'll try to express enough milk for you to keep in the freezer here." Camille asks if the mother will be able to come to the center and nurse the baby during her lunch hour. The mother answers, "There shouldn't be any problem with my coming every day. At least I'm going to try for a while." The new mother continues to talk to Camille while Carmelita moves around, responding to the other infants who have arrived. Several of the babies are now becoming fussy and, since Camille is still occupied with the new mother, the extra, or floating, assistant (who is the substitute whenever a staff member is absent and who generally helps where she is needed at other times) comes in to help in the infant area.

Carmelita sits on the floor watching and talking to two seven-month-old babies who are crawling on the carpet. One of the babies pushes herself to a sitting position and pulls a hat onto her head. The hat covers her face. She pulls hard on the brim of the hat but it comes down further over her face. She rocks up onto her knees, shakes her body, and begins to whimper. Carmelita leans over, pulls the hat back revealing the baby's face, and says, "Peek-a-boo." The baby laughs and rocks her body, causing the hat to fall down again over her eyes. Carmelita pulls the hat up and repeats, "Peek-a-boo." They laugh as this game is repeated several times. The other baby crawls closer and watches intently.

It is just after nine. In the next room all except one of the eight explorers have arrived for the day. Cissy, an assistant wearing blue jeans and t-shirt, is on her knees by the platform climbing structure with a 13-month-old who is climbing the little stairs. Cissy says, "Whoa, do you need some help, Chris?" She takes Chris's hand and steadies him as he maneuvers the stairs. Once he is on the platform, he lets go of Cissy's hand and grasps the rail with both hands. He leans toward Cissy and laughs as he reaches out to touch her shirt. She picks up a teddy bear from the floor and gently touches him on the nose with the bear as she says in a very high voice, "I love you, I love you, says the teddy bear." The child takes the teddy bear and toddles to the other end of the platform. He lies down on his stomach and slowly slides down the ramp, still holding the bear.

Christina, the teacher, is checking children's diapers. She bends down in front of Clarice and says, "How about if I change your diaper, okay?" Christina nuzzles Clarice on the cheek as she picks her up and says, "C'mon, okay?" As Christina lays Clarice on the diapering pad, Clarice points to the wallpaper ducks and says, "Yiee h duhee [light and ducky]." Then she twists around and reaches the light switch; she flips it on and off several times. Christina says, "Quack, quack, quack. Duck. Light, light. Where's the light?" Clarice points to the switch and answers, "Yiee." Christina lifts Clarice and hugs her, then puts her on the floor with a pat on the bottom. Christina writes on the chart, then continues checking diapers.

Craig, a 17-month-old boy, walks to her, whining and pulling up his shirt. He has several pink bumps along his waistline. Christina examines the bumps closely and says, "Is that uncomfortable? Let me take care of it, okay?" She turns to Cissy and, holding up Craig's shirt, says, "What is this on him?" Cissy says, "I don't know. I'm sure he didn't have it yesterday." Christina writes on Craig's chart, then gets ointment and a cotton swab. Craig resists having the ointment put on his rash so Christina says, "Here, you may have a swab to hold too. Isn't that interesting?" Then while Craig examines the swab, Christina quickly applies the ointment then says, "Okay, let's throw our swabs in the trash can. Thank you."

Just before ten, a mother wearing designer jeans and a stylishly oversized shirt comes into the explorers' classroom with her 14-month-old daughter, Cynde. As the mother takes the child's jacket off and puts her things away, she chats with Christina. She says, "We took Cynde to a restaurant last night. She got into this thing where she absolutely would not let anyone even touch her silverware. She was determined to feed herself." Christina says, "Oh that's terrific." The mother continues, "She had food everywhere. The waiters kept coming by and just smiling, but she had a fantastic time." They laugh. Christina says, "Yes, we're thinking of having a fire hydrant installed in the kitchen so we can clean up after lunch. But, you know, we're really big on independence."

By ten, the one-year-olds are clustered at the half-door to the kitchen. One is slapping the door. Another is trying to reach the doorknob. Christina says, "Oh God, we have a mutiny on our hands. I hope snack's ready. Cissy edges carefully through the babies, saying, "Excuse me! Excuse me, please. I need to get through the door, please. Thank you." The floating assistant arrives to help with snack, and the children are herded around to the end of the kitchen where there is a child-sized sink. The children are helped to wash their hands one at a time. The warm water running from the faucet is pleasant and the soap bubbles interesting, so the children are urged by Christina, "Oh yes, I think your hands are very clean. Would you like to dry them now so Craig can have a turn?"

The one-year-olds are guided to chairs and tiny paper plates of food are placed in front of them as soon as they are seated. There are pie-shaped segments of unsalted rice cakes with apple butter and cut pieces of banana with the peels still on them. The peelings have been cut on one side and a corner pulled up slightly so that the children can easily peel their own banana pieces. Craig picks up a banana piece and tries to bite into the peeling. Christina holds out her hands and, with an amused look of wonder, says, "Uh oh, what's wrong with your banana? Did you forgot to take the peeling off. Here, may I help you. Let's pull this part. Peeling, yuk, don't eat peeling. Ummm! Banana. Much better!"

Clarice holds up her arm toward Christina, opening and closing her hand, and says, "Teeah mo [Christina more]." Christina leans over with a plate of rice cakes and says, "More please. Can you say 'more please'?" Clarice says, "Mo pee [more please]," as she is served another piece. Cissy has poured a little apple juice into each of eight tiny paper cups. To each child she says, "Would you like some juice," as she places a cup beside each paper plate. Chris takes a sip, pours juice onto the paper plate, crushes the cup, then drops it on the floor. Cissy says, "Oops! On the floor. Uh oh, all finished." Chris gleefully pats the apple juice in his plate, splattering juice onto the table. Cissy takes the plate, saying, "I think you must be finished." Chris whimpers "Mo, mo" as he holds out his hand and kicks his chair. Christina gets another cup of juice and squats beside Chris. With her face close to his, she says softly but firmly, "May I help you with your juice, Chris?" He takes several sips, then Christina says, "Where does the cup go? Can you throw it in the trash can?" Christina holds his hand and walks with him to the trash. He drops the cup in the can and leans over to look inside.

The children are helped to wash and dry their hands again as each one finishes snack. Christina tells Cissy, "It's still pretty windy outside. Let's work in the classroom for a while. I'm going to give Clarice her medicine." She walks Clarice back to the diapering area and gets a bottle of red liquid from her cubby. It is labeled Sudafed and marked with Clarice's name. Clarice watches as Christina marks the time and date on a medicine chart then pours liquid into a plastic measuring tube. Christina kneels in front of Clarice and says, "I need to give you your medicine, Clarice." Christina holds the medicine to Clarice's lips. Clarice grimaces but swallows it. Christina says, "I know it's the pits, but I would like to see you breathe for a while. Let's blow your nose." Christina takes a tissue from a box and, in a slow and exaggerated manner, pretends to blow her own nose. Then she offers a clean tissue to Clarice and coaches, "That's it. Use two hands." Clarice gingerly wipes at her nose smearing mucous across her face. Christina says, "May I help you? There, now your nose is all clean. All clean!" Clarice holds up her hands and says, "Ah keen [all clean]."

The glass sliding doors are opened between the two explorers' areas. Cissy goes into the area with the climbing platform and Christina goes into the area with tables and chairs. Cissy sits on the floor and opens a book. Chris and two other children try to sit on her lap at the same time. Cissy pats the floor and says, "Sit down right here. There's room for you right here by me, Chris." Then she turns the pages slowly, pointing to pictures and saying, "Dog. Say Doggy. Ruff! Ruff! Doggy says ruff, ruff." The children crowd onto her lap.

In the other room, Christina has opened one of the closed shelves and placed four small rugs on the floor. She helps children as they pull materials off the shelves, guiding each to a different rug. She says, "Clarice, let's put your work here on this rug so nobody will bother you. Sit, please. Sit, please. That's it. Here's your work." She sits on the floor in front of the shelf within reach of the four rugs.

Craig shrieks when another child crawls onto his rug and takes his coffee can full of wooden clothes pins. Christina says, "Craig, use words. Please. Say 'my work, my work'." Christina gently restrains the other child, saying, "Craig says this is his work. Let's find your work. Here's your work. Shall we put it back and get new work?" Christina gathers three large yellow wooden beads and a fat yellow plastic spoon and puts them back in a yellow plastic dog dish. She dramatically lifts a yellow bead with the spoon from one side of the dish and says, "Up, up, up! Clunk! Down in the other side." She drops the bead off the spoon into the other side of the dish. The child takes the spoon and picks up a bead, puts it into the spoon, then picks it up from the spoon and drops it into the dish. Christina laughs and says, "Terrific! You did it."

The one-year-olds scatter pieces of their work, mouth them, and explore the physical properties of each. A 15-month-old girl named Celeste plays with a thick rubber peg board with nine holes in it. There are three red, three yellow, and three blue pegs. She pulls the fist-sized pegs out of the holes and drops them on her rug. She puts one peg in her mouth then picks up several in her hands, looks at them, then throws them. Christina gathers the pegs from other rugs and from under the shelf and says, "Celeste, your work goes on your rug. No throwing work, please. May I help you?" Christina notices the lump in Celeste's cheek. "Do you have work in your mouth? Apples and crackers are for eating. Work is not for eating." As Celeste spits out the peg, Christina says, "Thank you."

Celeste attempts to shove the peg into a hole in the board. It does not go in. She stands up with a peg in each hand and wanders to the other classroom. Cissy is still reading books on the floor. Celeste watches for a minute then walks over to the climbing structure. She inadvertently drops a peg onto the wooden stair. It spins for a second. Her mouth drops open as she stares at the spinning peg. When it stops, she picks it up. She examines it carefully, tastes it, then throws it down on the carpet. The peg lands with a soft thud but does not spin.

Celeste looks at the peg, picks it up, then throws it again onto the carpet. It does not spin. She frowns, picks it up, walks toward Cissy, whimpers then throws it down again. Still it does not spin. She bites the peg hard then drops it on the floor and walks to Christina in the back classroom, whimpering and shaking her head. Christina steps to the door and says, "Cissy, could you get Celeste a bottle, she's really getting fussy." Cissy brings a baby bottle of apple juice from the kitchen and takes Celeste to the pillow on the floor. Celeste rests on the soft pillow, clutching a stuffed animal and sucking her bottle.

At eleven the cook steps into the classroom and signals Christina that lunch is ready. Christina says, "Let's put our work away," as she gathers and returns the materials to the shelf that he children have been using. She stands, closes the shelf, and stacks the little rugs. Craig and Clarice drag rugs to her and she says, "Oh good. You're helping put work away." Then Christina walks to the kitchen half-door, clapping her hands softly and saying in rhythm to the claps, "Time for lunch. Time for lunch."

Lunch takes place just as snack did, except that hot foods and spoons are provided. Several of the 12- and 13-month-old children use only their fingers to feed themselves. One holds the spoon in his left hand as he picks up food with his right hand. The adults stand at alert around the tables, providing assistance and more food and drink as the children indicate.

The first child who is finished is guided to throw her paper plate and cup away and helped to wash her hands. Cissy escorts her to the diapering area, changes her and gives her a bottle as she lies down on a plastic nap mat that has been covered with a floral pillowcase. Cissy spreads a little blanket over her, pats her for a minute, then hurriedly arranges the other seven mats around the room. She knows which pillowcase belongs to each child and exactly what items they need for nap. She places a teddy bear and a pacifier on one, a plush blanket, a bottle of milk, and a rag doll on another. Christina and the cook send children in to lie down as soon as their lunch is finished and their hands are washed. Most of the children go directly to their own mats. A few lie down. Cissy talks to them softly as she changes diapers.

Christina comes in with the last child and speaking in a whisper says, "I need to see you lying down. Lie down please." She sits between Craig and Chris and pats their backs as she whispers directions to other children. Celeste begins to cry softly as she rubs her eyes and yawns. Cissy carries her to her mat, patting her and saying, "It's time for nap." Celeste cries and resists when Cissy attempts to lay her on the mat. Cissy sits down on the floor beside the mat and rocks Celeste in her lap. Celeste's whimpering subsides and her eyes close so Cissy eases her gently onto the mat and covers her with her baby blanket. In 30 minutes most of the children are asleep and Christina leaves for her lunch break. Cissy sits and pats children until the last few are asleep. She then gets a drink from the kitchen and relaxes against a wall, sipping her soda and staring at the sleeping one-year-olds.

By the time the children begin waking, several morning staff members have left for the day and an afternoon teacher and several afternoon assistants have arrived. Before Christina leaves she tells her afternoon assistants, "If Celeste cries when she wakes up just hold her. Carry her around until she wriggles to get down. I know it's tough but it will be worth it in the long run. Listen, I've been with them all morning. It's only Monday and look here, dotted lines on both wrists—'cut here'." The assistants laugh with Christina then one asks, "Won't that make her, you know, what do you call, hecharse a perder?" The other assistant says, "She means spoiled." Christina says, "No, no. Spoiling is great. Spoiling makes you a real survivor."

As soon as each child wakes, he or she is changed and escorted outside to the playground. Two assistants continue to talk about whether or not carrying babies will spoil them as they help babies to swing, play in the sandbox, ride tiny tricycles, and climb on a low outdoor climbing structure. At three o'clock, the explorers are brought inside. Afternoon snack is served and the children are escorted to the classrooms again to be changed and to do their work with the learning materials, books, and climbing equipment. Within an hour parents begin arriving for their children.

At five-thirty, Craig's mother comes in, greets him then says to the afternoon teacher, "Will you tell Christina and Camille that we are interested in setting up a conference to talk about Craig moving to the cottage. He will be 18 months old next week and we understand that the children move from the infant school to the cottage when they are 18 months old." The teacher assures Craig's mother that the staff would be happy to schedule a parent conference. She also tells the mother that Christina will schedule certain mornings for Cissy to take Craig to the cottage and stay with him for one-hour visits but that children are not actually moved until teachers and directors from both schools agree that Craig is ready. By the time they leave, it is six o'clock and time for the staff to lock the doors.

The Cottage

At seven o'clock in the morning, Carla Caruthers opens the building that the Color-Coordinated Country Day School staff and the parents refer to as the cottage. It is located about four blocks from the infant school. The cottage houses children from about 18 months to 36 months of age. It is adjacent to another much larger building, which is also owned by Color-Coordinated Country Day School, called the preprimary school for children three, four, and five years old.

The cottage is a New England-style frame house with a wide front porch and two large bay windows on the front of the building and a row of french doors leading to a spacious deck on the back. There is an old-fashioned black wrought-iron fence in front and a high wooden fence in back. The front door has a number-coded lock on it like that on the infant school.

The two main areas in the building are two classrooms, one for younger toddlers and one for older. Just inside the front door is a large open space that is the classroom for 24- to 36-month-old children. Sunny window seats in the two bay windows hold lush hanging and potted plants. The floor has beige carpeting except for an area of vinyl tile in an alcove off the right side of the classroom. Two walls of the carpeted area are lined with low wooden shelves.

The shelves have carefully spaced rows of color-coordinated objects that are designed as learning activities. The materials are organized into categories, with each shelf designated as a specific area of learning. While at first glance the objects appear to be simple games and toys, their arrangement designates the teachers' underlying purpose for each item.

A doll and blanket in a wooden cradle and a toy service station complete with cars, tow trucks, and gas pumps are both placed with the language area, since play with them tends to involve speech and the manipulation of symbolic objects. A set of little cups and saucers is placed in the math area since matching cups to saucers is a kind of one-to-one correspondence. Plastic fruits and vegetables with matching picture cards are placed in the science area, little pitchers of water for practice in pouring are placed in the practical life area, and marking pens and paper are placed in the art area. Materials are assigned to content areas by the subjective rationale of staff members. There is a fluid overlapping in these assignments; teachers may name cups-and-saucers a practical life activity rather than a math activity, or pens-and-paper a language activity rather than an art activity, but once named, every individual item in every set of materials is assigned to a given spot on a given shelf. The color-coding simplifies the maintenance of this designated organization.

In the tiled alcove, there are two shelves of materials; two low tables with 12 tiny chairs; a very low sink with soap, paper towels, and sponges in the children's reach; and a large basin containing cups, funnels, water toys, and a small plastic pitcher. On the floor beside the low basin is a plush rug to soak up spills. High on the walls are storage shelves for the teachers. Beside the sink is a door that leads to the younger children's classroom.

At the left end of the two-year-olds' classroom is a door that leads to a restroom with two sinks, two toilets, and high shelves holding stacks of disposable diapers labeled with children's names. The two child-sized toilets are side by side without any partitions between them. One of the sinks is a deep janitor-type fixture with a spray faucet for bathing toddlers when bowel-movement accidents require extensive cleaning. The other is a small bathroom sink mounted about a foot off the floor to be available to even the smallest children. Soap, paper towels, and a tiny wastebasket are within reach, and a large covered container is available for soiled diapers. Doors open from the restroom to both of the classrooms. Adjacent to the restroom is a coat closet with low coat hooks and cubbyholes that also opens to both classrooms.

The younger toddlers' classroom, for children 18 to 24 months, is designed and arranged very much like the first classroom. Similar games and toys have been selected, with most having fewer and slightly larger pieces. The basin in this room has fewer cups and and funnels, but it is still designed for the children to use independently. The classroom is shaped differently, but it still has carpeted and tiled areas. The materials are different, but they are divided into essentially the same content areas. One difference from the other classroom is the addition of equipment for large-muscle activity. A tunnel made of a barrel mounted on a wooden base is placed at one end of the carpeted area beside a tiny set of climbing stairs. The classroom overlooks the deck and back playground. Past the classroom is a small kitchen.

The children's day in the cottage is scheduled much like the explorers' day in the infant school. Lunch, snack, and nap times are adapted to the children's needs. The rest of the day is generally divided into indoor and outdoor times that are determined by the weather and the children's interest. One difference in the cottage is that once or twice a day the children sit down on the carpet together for a few minutes of group activity.

By eight o'clock in the morning, the classroom for the younger children is full of movement and sound. Carla, their teacher, and two assistants quietly attend to the children, moving among the children, sitting with them, and talking to them. Nine of the 12 children in the class are present, and Carla greets parents and children as others arrive. A few of the children cry for a few minutes when their parents leave. Many come in with a smile and hurry to choose work from the shelf to play with. Almost as many fathers as mothers deliver children. Carla helps children remember to put their work on little rugs that are intended to define territory and property rights.

Two girls struggle over a doll bottle. One squeals loudly. Carla quietly moves to them and says, "Conny, use words. Say 'my work'." Then she looks at Crystal and says, "Crystal, here is your rug. You need to play with your work. This is Conny's work." Crystal pulls at the bottle again and cries, "My, my [mine]!" She pulls at Conny's hair and Conny squeals again. Carla quickly takes Crystal's hand away from Conny's hair and says, "Oh, ouch, pulling hurts. Please, no hurting. Use words. Use words." Crystal continues to cry as she repeats, "My, my!" Carla gently takes Conny's hand and says, "Crystal feels very sad. She says the bottle is hers. Would you like a different bottle?" Carla quickly gets a different doll bottle from a shelf and says, "May I trade with you?" Carla gives Conny the new bottle and holds her hand out for the trade. Conny stares at both bottles and at Carla's outstretched hand. Finally, she puts the contested bottle in Carla's hand. Carla hands the bottle to Crystal, then pats and praises Conny, saying, "How nice of you to share with your friend Crystal."

One boy who appears tired is helped to a mat in a quiet corner. He falls asleep immediately. Periodically through the day, the teacher and assistants check diapers and ask, "Do you need to use the toilet?" Children who need changing are escorted to the restroom and helped out of their clothes, washed, and changed while standing. Each child is always asked to do as much as he or she is able in getting pants up and down. They are coaxed, "Hold your blue jeans here and pull. Would you like for me to pull the back? Great, now you've almost got them. Pull hard. Good."

When it is time for snack the children put much of their work away independently. An assistant stands by the sink ready to help while children wash and dry their own hands. When one child becomes fascinated with the liquid soap, the assistant says, "One squirt please. Thank you." The children climb into chairs and gleefully pound on the tables with their hands as Carla serves them food. They eat as soon as they are served. One child is still playing with a little farm house and toy animals. Carla says, "Carl, would you like some snack?" He shakes his head and says, "No nah [snack]. No wah [want] nah. Pay [play] cah [cars] Cado [Carla]. He runs a toy tractor up the wall. Carla smiles and pats him as she says, "Here, go on the table, that's the wall." He continues his activity while the other children eat snack. As children finish their snacks, they are helped to scrape their own plates and put them in a basin. One 18-month-old girl gets a sponge from the sink and spends several minutes wiping at a table.

At ten-thirty the doors to the deck are opened and children crowd outside to play with the wooden wagon, wheelbarrow, and riding toys. One assistant stays inside with several children who have chosen not to go outside. At eleven-thirty, the children come back inside, and Carla claps her hands chanting in rhythm, "Time for circle, time for circle." Children come and sit on the carpet in some semblance of a circle. Conny drags a chair to the group and says, "Dis [this] is cheers [chairs]." Carla answers, "Yes, Conny's chair. Do you need some help?" The adults sit on the floor, cross-legged, as the children sit with feet stuck straight out in front of them. Conny sits on a chair holding a picture book.

Carla notices a small red block on the carpet that has been dropped by one of the children. She picks it up and holds it in her closed hands saying, "Here is the box, here is the lid, I wonder whatever inside could be hid." She makes a little gasping sound as she says brightly, "Oh, it's a cube. Crystal, would you like to put it away for us?" Then she says, "Can you catch a bumblebee? Okay. Let's sing our song." The children clasp their hands and move in rhythm as Carla sings, "I'm bringing home a baby bumblebee, won't my daddy be so proud of me. I'm bringing home a baby bumblebee. Open the window, bye, bye, baby bumblebee. Fly away home." Some of the children are able to sing a few of the words, but most of the children are animated in making the movements and gestures that go with the song. Carla leads the children in singing "The Wheels on the Bus." All of the children become very quiet as they touch their lips and sing in a whisper, "The mommies on the bus say shhhh, shhhh, shhhh."

The older toddler class has had a morning similar to the younger toddlers except that the children are much more adept at getting out, concentrating on, and putting away their work. Also, more of them do their work in pairs and trios rather than alone or alongside another child. Most of the older toddlers are out of diapers and are able to go to the bathroom with little or no help. They are willing to sit still longer than the younger toddlers, so when they have group time, they hear a story in addition to singing songs. As Cora, the older toddler's teacher, reads a book to the group clustered around her, she points to a picture of a train and says, "What color is that train?" Several children answer "blue." Cora says, "Yes, it's a blue train. Is that a new train or an old train?" Simultaneously, a girl says old and a boy says new. Cora says, "Yes, it's an old train." The boy loudly says, "No! New!" Cora asks, "Is it new? I think it's old." The boy again says, "No! New!" Cora looks at the picture of the old blue train and quietly says, "Oh, new." She continues reading the story.

After the group activity, children again choose materials with which to work. One boy spends a long period of time playing with water toys in the plastic basin adjacent to the sink area. He slowly fills and pours out containers of water, stopping occasionally to look in the small, framed mirror mounted on the wall in front of him. The only black child in the center is a two-year-old girl named Chirrika. She sits on the carpet looking at a picture book as Charles sits down beside her and puts his hand on her book. She says, "No, no. Mine." He removes his hand and says, "I show you. I show you." She repeats, "No, no. Mine." Charles puts his hands behind him as he leans close and says, "Read it." Chirrika looks at him quizzically and says, "I can't." Charles leaves as she continues turning the pages of her book. Cynthia sits down by Chirrika and takes hold of the book. Chirrika shoves Cynthia away. Cynthia shrieks and yells, "Don't do dat [that]." Chirrika parrots, "Do dat" as she gently shoves Cynthia again. The assistant teacher quickly arrives saying, "Be careful, please." Cynthia says, "Don't do dat," and Chirrika answers, "Mine, mine." The adult kneels down with one hand on each child's head. She says softly, "This is Chirrika and this is Cynthia. Chirrika has a sweater and Cynthia has a shirt. This book belongs to Chirrika. Cynthia, would you like to cut with scissors?" Cynthia holds hands with the assistant teacher and they walk to the art shelf to get scissors.

The morning work period is almost over when a mother comes in the front door with a two-year-old boy. She looks at Cora and apologetically says, "I couldn't get him to go to sleep no matter what I did last night. Midnight! I even threatened him. I said if you don't go to sleep...." Her voice trails off as she watches her son put his things in his cubby. Then she looks at him and says, "Would you like to wear your Mickey Mouse shirt so when you go outside you'll have something on your head?" Without looking at her the boy firmly says no. She answers, "No? Okay. Bye. Can I have a kiss?" They kiss and as she leaves, she pauses to watch her son play with a blanket and a doll bed. She says, "Oh, are you the daddy? Good boy." Then she leaves.

Chirrika and Cynthia have made friends again and are playing with a large wooden puzzle that consists of graduated rings that fit on a large peg. Cynthia says, "You want dis one. Dis heaby [heavy] one. Dis one bik [big]. Hode [hold it] wi [with] two hands. You play dis. Den [then] I put onna [on the] rug. No! put onna cake." Then she sings, "Happy birtay [birthday] to you," repeating the song several times as Chirrika watches. Chirrika reaches for a wooden ring and Cynthia snaps, "You can't do dis. No! Mine! You wan [want] me help you?" Chirrika takes her hand away from the toy and sings with Cynthia, "Appy [happy] to you." Cynthia says, "Eat cake. Bwow [blow] cannows [candles]. C'mon, C'mon. Time to lunch." She repeats herself several times then asks, "You like it? Eat dis." Chirrika answers, "Yea." Cynthia grabs the wooden disk out of Chirrika's hand and says, "We has to cook it." Chirrika leaves and goes to cut with scissors.

From across the room there is the sound of two boys chasing and screaming. In a shocked voice, Cora says, "Please, can you use words? Say 'may I play'." The assistant comes into the room and quietly announces, "C'mon. It's time for lunch. Time for lunch."

After lunch, Cora helps the children get ready for nap. She asks one little girl who is still in diapers to use the toilet and the girl replies softly, "No, Cowah [Cora], maybe 'morrow." Cora says, "Would you like to watch the other children?" The child shakes her head and Cora smiles and says, "When you're ready, you let me know, okay? Maybe tomorrow, right?"

While the assistant helps with the children who are ready to lie down on their mats, Cora helps three boys who are in the restroom. As they use the toilets, she ties shut a small plastic garbage bag of soiled diapers. Charles asks, "I hep [help]?" Cora thanks him and hands him the bag. As he walks out into the classroom, Cynthia says, "I hep too." She squeals and chases him but he refuses to give the bag to her. Cora offers Cynthia a second bag and she struts through the room with it. Corey, Charles' best friend, looks at Charles and says, "I hep you?" Charles grins and offers the bag saying, "Yes, we share." Corey looks at Cora with a big grin and says, "He say I share." Charles grins and says, "We got gabrige [garbage]. We got beek [big] shtron [strong] hands." Corey laughs and pats the bag saying, "It got poots." Charles says, "We share. We soo beek help." They follow Cynthia and Cora out the door as they carry the bags to a garbage container behind the kitchen.

At the end of the day, parents can look at each child's chart, not only to see if the child has had success with the toilet during the day, but also to see a description of the specific materials and activities the child worked with during the day. Before the doors are locked at closing time, the teachers and assistants go through the contents of each shelf in the school straightening, sorting out any pieces that have been mixed, and checking to see that every piece of every set is present. Any set with a part missing is removed to a teachers' storage and work area until the missing piece is replaced or repaired.

At six o'clock, the lights are turned off and the doors are bolted for the night.

Le Exclusive Enfants School

An Epilogue

Le Exclusive Enfants School is a renovated storefront building located adjacent to a fashionable shopping mall by a freeway in a heavily populated metropolitan area. Shoppers walking by the front of the building can see children in school uniforms sitting at tables working with attractive young women in uniform school smocks. Just inside the front door is an elegant office and reception area. Tasteful art prints of works from the French impressionist period dot the walls, and the soft hum of elevator-type music softens the sounds of children from the classrooms.

Glass walls on the right end of the building make it possible to look from many of the classrooms into an elaborate enclosed garden that serves as the playground. Virtually all of the enclosed area is covered in wooden decking, planter boxes, or play structures. Glass doors open directly from the classrooms.

A hallway leads from the center of the building to a large classroom area at the far left end of the building that is used for children from one to 18 months of age. The area is divided into three parts, one each for the babies, the crawlers, and the walkers. The first two parts each have rows of nine elegant and expensive designer cribs at the back and open, carpeted play areas in the front. Low partitions divide each of the areas so that children are confined to the three sections, but the room appears to be one large, open environment. The third section, for the oldest babies, has one large, low table with 11 small chairs. Rows of high chairs for feeding, a large wicker toy box, two wooden riding toys, 11 nap mats, a diapering area, and a learning materials storage area complete the furnishings.

The other two sections, for the babies and the crawlers, are equipped in an almost identical manner. Besides the cribs, each has a wicker basket of toys, three board and bracket shelves, out of the reach of the children, that hold stuffed animals and picture books, and several automatic swings with winding devices. Each has a diapering area with cubbyholes. Sanitary paper and disposable gloves are available for diaper changes and each soiled disposable diaper is individually wrapped before it is thrown away.

Teacher supply areas hold various sets of large, carefully constructed flash cards. Math training with flash cards begins at eight months. Reading training with flash cards begins at 11 months. Video equipment is available in a specially designed studio in the middle of the center to record for parents the performances of their children in work and play activities.

Each of the three groups has one caregiver who holds some type of teacher certification and is responsible for teaching the children. Each group also has an aide who is responsible for "diapers, lunch, and noses." A fourth aide, the floater, moves from area to area as needed.

At nine o'clock in the morning, Emily, the teacher for the middle group, greets a mother and her seven-month-old daughter, Elise. Elise pulls at Emily's hair and smiles at her. The mother says, "I ran out of medicine sheets but she still needs medicine at eleven and three." There is the sound of crying behind Emily and she turns and says firmly, "Erin and Eloise!" She takes the wicker basket of toys and dumps it in front of Erin saying, "Play with Eloise. No! Here, play over here." Emily shakes her index finger at Erin and says, "Be nice or I'll put you in the swing." She turns back to the mother and says, "They usually don't cry like this."

Erin continues to whimper and grab toys. Emily checks the chart then says, "I think I've found the solution to this little baby's crying. Do you want some juice?" She hands Erin a bottle of juice and he begins to crawl away holding the nipple in his teeth. Emily says, "Uhhh uhhh! Go sit down. Do you want us to take it away?" Then she laughs at him as she whisks him to a sitting position, saying, "Sit down Erin the Barbarian. Sit down."

Esther, the teacher for the youngest group, goes to the crib area to pick up a four-month-old baby who has awakened. She puts the baby in a swing to protect her from the other, larger babies. It is time for lessons so Esther places Edie in a sitting position on the carpet and holds up large flash cards with one to ten red dots on each in a random pattern. Esther gets Edie's attention then begins, changing flash cards as she says each number, "One, two, three...." Edie smiles and reaches for the cards, trying to pull them into her mouth. Esther firmly plants her in a sitting position and says, "Look here Edie. Good! Good girl! Look at the cards. One, two, three...." Esther quickly gets to ten and pats Edie on the head again, praising her and then giving her a toy off the shelf.

The next child to get a lesson is a boy who has been doing the cards for several weeks. Esther places him on the floor and begins the routine. He snaps his head away from Esther and her cards. She lays the cards down saying, "Okay, you don't want to do them today?" He immediately looks back, but each time she holds up the cards, he looks in the opposite direction. Esther gets up and goes to another child. This child sits looking at each of the cards. She bounces her body in time to the teacher's words and points her little index finger at some of the cards as they go by. At one point she leans forward on her knees and tries to look at the cards beside Esther. Esther quickly slides the cards behind her back and blocks the child's view of them by holding the cards immediately in front of the girl's eyes. The girl sits back up and looks around.

In the area for the oldest group of babies, the teacher, the aide, and the floater have gotten all of the children sitting down at the table. The teacher, Esmeralde, says in a strong Spanish accent, "Ellis, get down from the table. Shame on you. That is not a nice thing for you to do. Seet down, please, children." She then dumps a small pile of little blocks in front of each child and says, "No! No throwing blocks. Stop it, okay?" Several children stare at the blocks, one continues throwing, and the rest begin building. Esmeralde says, "Good! Good!," and claps her hands each time a child stacks any of the blocks. After a few more minutes of play, the aide whisks the blocks away and brings the group's flash cards. Several of the children slap the table with their hands. The aide says, "No, no."

From the areas of the younger babies there is the loud sound of many babies crying and an adult with an exasperated voice saying, "Stop it! Stop crying!" Esmeralde glances across the room at the crying babies as she places a paper in front of each child. Several crawlers from the next area have pulled up and are standing at the low partition watching the proceedings at the table. Each of the children at the table has a sheet of paper with his or her name on it, a drawing of a triangle, and the printed word, triangle. As children are handed fat crayons, almost all immediately put the crayons in their mouths. All three adults go around the table, holding each child's hand in turn and making the crayon in each child's hand color the triangle on his or her paper. As they go they all say, "Not in your mouth. Do not put that in your mouth." Esmeralde says, "It's hot in here. Edgar, take it out of your mouth."

Edgar pulls up the vinyl table cloth and hides his head. When the aide pulls him out and replaces the table cloth, he grabs his paper and crushes it. Esmeralde says, "Oh Edgar, your master-piece. No! No!" The papers are quickly cleared and Esmeralde carries the flash cards around the table placing each card directly in front of each child's eyes. The first card has the word eye on it. As she goes to each child, she says, "Show me your eye. Where is your eye? Good!"

Edgar sits with his elbows on the table. He lays his cheek on his forearm then vigorously rubs his eyes with his fists. He looks away when Esmeralde reaches him with the flash cards. The aide comes to the table bringing cartons of Play-Doh. Esmeralde says, "No, let's give them snack and then take them outside. They're getting tired. They've worked hard this morning." Little paper cups of juice and some crackers are placed in front of the children. After the children have had snack, the adults clear the table then escort them to the outdoor play area. The director stands at the door as the children come through. She says to the teachers and aides, "It looks like you are all being really patient today."

As the children come through the older children's classrooms, they pass a group of 18- through 24-month-old children who are taking their French lesson. A young French-speaking woman is sitting on a chair with a circle of 12 toddlers. Today is her first day at Le Exclusive Enfants. She says in a very thick French accent, "I cannot see. That is because everybody is standing up. I wish everybody would sit down. Go to your chair! Seet down! You can see the peecture but I do not want you to touch it."

Just past the French lesson is an area where toddlers are milling comfortably around a wooden slide. A teacher who is changing a little girl's clothes in one corner calls to them, "No, no. Don't get on the slide. Leave the toys alone. We are getting ready for class. Evelyn, we do not hit our friends!"

Eventually, all of the 18- through 24-month-olds are herded into an area with tables for work similar to that done with the walking babies except that the group size is larger and more materials are placed in front of the children over a longer period of time. When the teacher leaves for her break and is replaced by a floater, a little girl leaves the table and runs after her. She stops and says, "Go back. You have to go back to the tables. You aren't supposed to be out here, okay?" She sees the little girl's disappointed look and she says, "Okay, give me a kiss then go back." She kisses the little girl, they hug and smile, then the teacher waves goodbye and leaves. The floater comes out and escorts the girl back to her place at the table.

VI

FINDINGS

In the social sciences we stand, like Newton,
on a beach of sand, looking first at this
pebble or this shell, while a sea of truth lay
undiscovered before us. [Lubeck 1985]

Educators, sociologists, and anthropologists have long tried to comprehend and explain vast cultural differences in human behavior. Sadly predictable patterns of school failure and poverty are somehow perpetuated in the lowest levels of socioeconomic strata, and equally predictable patterns of school success and affluence are perpetuated at the higher levels. Bernstein and others have theorized that certain parental and educational practices solidify the status quo and pass the patterns of socioeconomic status from one generation to the next. Schools have been theorized to both represent and reproduce existing class and economic divisions in the society as a whole.

Findings from this study affirm the presence of such processes and assert that these cultural mechanisms for social reproduction begin in infancy. Further, findings indicate that parents unwittingly participate in social reproduction through differential enculturation, not only in direct interactions with their children but also by seeking out and employing caregivers outside the home whose ideologies related to child-rearing generally match those held by the parents. Also, apparently, these ideologies, perceptions of meaning, linguistic codes, and patterns of interaction evolve from and are directly related to each adult participant's interpretation of social and cultural reality.

The present study used infant/toddler day care centers as lenses through which to view an important new phenomenon in human socialization—the daily care of infants and toddlers in proprietary group settings. Center A served a working-class, relatively low-income clientele; center B, a middle-class clientele with modest incomes; center C, a highly educated professional clientele with affluent means; and center E, an executive elite clientele with affluent means. During the course of this study, the verbal interaction between adults and children was a constant focal point.

Children from one to three years of age are generally considered by child developmentalists to be in the most fertile period of language learning they will ever experience. A commonly known phenomenon is the process whereby young children in a foreign country learn the native language more quickly and more perfectly than their parents. Bernstein theorizes that language, in terms of linguistic code, mediates and is mediated by one's perception of meaning and one's perceived social role. Surely the language of caregivers who share a majority of children's waking hours has an impact on the children's enculturation and on their development of values, meanings, roles, and culture-specific behaviors.

Language in the centers varied dramatically—from, for example, "Here, let me open the doe [door] so nobody won't fall out," to, "May I help you. I think that you may catapult onto your head."* Language was selected as a key indicator of socialization differences. Further, enculturation was looked at as a dialectical interaction rather than as a one-sided process of adults molding children.

The adult usage of linguistic code and social control strategies used in the centers was found to match the adults' interpretations of their own personal roles and experiences in the larger society. The folk ideologies of the four centers can be seen in the chart on the following page.

Linguistic Code

Elaborated and restricted linguistic codes can be identified by the use of literal or nonliteral statements, by the use of linguistic markers, and by the level of context-independence or dependence of meanings in statements. Bernstein [1971] describes how the elaborated linguistic code lends itself to highly differentiated and

---

*All speech quotations are from field notes.

CENTER C	CENTER E
Elaborated Linguistic Code	*Elaborated Linguistic Code*
literal speech linguistic markers context-independent meanings	literal speech linguistic markers context-independent meanings
Personal Social Control	*Positional Social Control*
cognitive-oriented appeal child-centered curriculum eqalitarian structure gender equity	mixed/imperatives and appeals adult-centered curriculum hierarchical structure some gender differentiation
CENTER B	**CENTER A**
Restricted Linguistic Code	*Restricted Linguistic Code*
nonliteral speech few linguistic markers context-dependent meanings	nonliteral speech few linguistic markers context-dependent meanings
Personal Social Control	*Positional Social Control*
mixed/imperatives and appeals child-centered curriculum egalitarian structure some gender differentiation	imperative commands adult-centered curriculum hierarchical structure marked gender differentiation

complex syntactical nuances often requiring the use of linguistic markers such as "uh" or "um" to allow the speaker time to formulate utterances. The restricted code produces a rigid, predictable folk syntax and repetitive phrases not conducive to the use of markers. Cryptic, nonliteral statements that are understood among kin and utterances that may be literal but cannot be understood unless the shared meaning of a specific context is known, are typical of restricted code usage. In the elaborated code, literal and context-independent communication is used since the speaker does not assume the existence of shared knowledge and context.

Nonliteral Expressions

Nonliteral statements were a regular part of social interactions in center A. Children were often asked, "Do you want to get in the corner?" A "yes" or "no" response to the literal question would have been deemed inappropriate and rude. The desired response to the question was simply a change in behavior.

One morning Mrs. Anderson discovered Ainetta on top of a table. She looked straight at Ainetta and said in an authoritative tone, "You are not on that table." When several children shouted, "Yes she is," Mrs. Anderson firmly repeated, "I do not see you on top of that table!" After a moment, Ainetta sheepishly crawled off.

Miss Beth, in center B, also tended to use nonliteral statements. When a one-year-old boy toddled out an open door into the kindergarten classroom, Miss Beth laughed and called out, "Get back in here or I'll kill you!" Miss Beth often exclaimed, "You're gonna split your head wide open and Miss Beth is gonna havta rush you to the hospital if you don't get off that thing." Sometimes her nonliteral comments were euphemistic and veiled threats, "Do you want to go night-night?" In centers A and B, words sometimes had contradictory meanings. Miss Betty sometimes said "okay" as praise and sometimes said the same word as a reprimand. Only her tone, inflection, and expression indicated which was intended.

In centers C and E, adults more often spoke in a literal manner. Cora said, "Please be careful. The floor is hard. It could hurt if you fall."

Linguistic Markers

Another indicator of the teachers' relative use of elaborated and restricted codes was their relative use of linguistic markers such as "uh" or "um." Turner and Pickvance [1973] have correlated these linguistic markers with the elaborated code, since periodic thinking time is required to plan complicated and unpredictable speech assemblies. In the restricted code, markers are not really needed since the speech tends to be limited to more regular and predictable word sequences.

Adult subjects in the study were observed for the use of linguistic markers both in day-to-day speech and during structured interviews. Generally, their usage was fairly consistent in both settings, but for comparison among centers, the occurrence of markers in tape-recorded responses to structured interview questions was actually counted. In these structured interviews Mrs. Aiken and Mrs. Anderson did not rely on markers. Mrs. Aiken was recorded saying "um" only once, and Mrs. Anderson not at all. Miss Beth used markers more than the center A teachers but less than any of the other teachers in the study. She was heard to say "um" or "uh" only five times.

Miss Betty used markers more than any other teacher given the structured interview questions, but she tended to use the markers as part of circular redundancy sequences (typical of restricted code usage). For example, one of her interview responses included the statement, "...and, um, you just, lot of times, you just, um, you can't do anything, I mean, there's just, uh, you can't do nothin' with 'em...." Her excessive use of markers seemed more an indication of nervousness than a need to plan the structure of utterances. General observations of Miss Betty indicated that her speech was less restricted than that of Miss Beth, but more restricted than that of Miss Bonnie. Miss Bonnie, the director of center B, used 13 markers and almost no redundancy sequences in her lengthy response to the structured interview questions.

Center C personnel consistently had lengthy responses with high usages of markers. Christina used 17 markers, Carla and Cora each used 25 markers. Carla used a number of circular redundancy sequences, but her meanings were more context independent and her grammar more standard than that used by Miss Betty. General observations supported the inference that Cora (director of center C) evidenced the highest level of speech elaboration of the subjects who responded to the structured interview questions. (Center E personnel were not asked structured interview questions but had a generally high usage of markers in day-to-day conversations.)

Context Embeddedness

An additional indication of elaboration is context independence. The interview responses of Miss Bonnie, Christina, Carla, and Cora are context-independent enough that one reading a transcript of their statements can understand precisely what the subjects perceived they would do and say. In most cases one can even infer the questions that have been asked. In the more context-dependent responses of center A and B subjects, the meaning of responses can only be understood if the context is known. For example, in response to the same question, Mrs. Aiken said, "Well, sometimes I makes 'em clean it up," while Cora said, "I go 'oops,' probably make a little song up about, you know, spilling milk and, uh, you know, invite them to come and help me get a paper towel and wet it and wipe the table and wipe the floor." In this example, the redundancy and specificity of Cora's response makes explicit the situation and what she would do and say. The meaning of Mrs. Aiken's response is implicit in the context of shared perception of meaning between the speaker and the listener.

Language differences in the centers were dramatic. Linguistic differences in adult subject responses to structured interview questions were stark compared to the literal content of the answers given, which tended to be fairly similar. Generally, all of the content of responses given could have been fitted into generic categories such as comfort, distract, praise, be firm, or explain to the child. Bernstein's theoretical structure, however, provides a highly effective scalpel to cut apart the responses and discern subtle but important cultural differences among them.

Social Control

Social control is a key area of resistance and accommodation for toddlers in their interaction with adults, and a critical area of socialization. Children from nine months to three years of age are in a unique stage of human development. Newly mastered motor skills make them mobile, but limited experience and comprehension make them vulnerable. One- and two-year-olds are notoriously accident prone, are oblivious of the rights of others, and cannot as yet inhibit impulses.

All of the centers had some method of isolating the children, as a way of dealing with misbehavior, although there were important differences among the centers. Mrs. Aiken sent children to stand in a corner, Miss Beth put children in a playpen, Cora removed children from problem situations, redirecting them toward other activities, and Esther put children in swings until they were "relaxed and calmed down." Although no punishment other than reprimanding or isolating was seen during the study, there were indications that the children in center A knew that a small wooden ruler kept on the teacher's table could be used for punishment.

One afternoon, Mrs. Anderson asked me to watch the children for a few minutes while she went next door. After she left I asked, "How do I watch you?" A three-year-old girl ran to the teacher's table and brought me the teacher's ruler. After she handed it to me,

I looked puzzled and said, "What should I do with this?" Annie, a two-year-old, snatched it from me and quickly slapped her hand with it several times saying, "Do dis [this]."

In center B, Miss Beth had only two playpens, so when more than two children were causing her problems, she employed distractions that usually consisted of crackers, juice, toys, or words such as, "Hey, hey, hey, look here!" Distractions were also used in center C, but they tended to be more subtle, for example, "Let's go look out of the window." In center E, one teacher repeatedly made loud, shrill, trilling sounds to distract babies and toddlers from their crying.

To focus on the daily socialization struggles between adults and these newly mobile children, data from participant observation and from structured interviews were examined using Cook-Gumperz's [1979] control strategies. Two categories were examined—imperatives, primarily a position-oriented strategy, and cognitive appeals, a person-oriented strategy. The study also examined how the personal or positional orientation impinged upon curriculum methodology, personnel working relationships, and gender stereotyping.

Imperatives and Cognitive Appeals

The use of imperatives or cognitive appeals was found not only to be tied to perceptions of personal or positional role relationships but somewhat related to one's linguistic code usage also. Imperatives, typical in positional modes of social control, were almost exclusively relied upon in center A where a restricted linguistic code prevailed, but were tempered with some use of cognitive appeals in center E where an elaborated linguistic code was primarily used. Cognitive appeals, typical in personal modes of social control, were almost exclusively relied upon in center C where the elaborated code was used, but were modified by the use of imperatives in center B where a restricted code was used.

Clearly, center C used cognitive appeals as a strategy for social control most frequently and imperative commands least frequently. For example, when two children fought over a book, Carla slowly and deliberately said, "Do you want to read a book? If you pull on the book, it may tear. Would you like for me to read you a book? What book do you want? Where do you want to sit?" When two children in center A fought over a book, Mrs. Aiken said, "Give that back! Why you wanta act like that?" Carla's response to the fight implies an expectation of logical, divergent thinking and decision making. Mrs. Aiken's response regulates a desired convergent action.

In center A, the adults maintained a teacherly tone, an imperative manner of speaking that would seem equally appropriate in a sixth grade arithmetic class. The teachers spoke to children in an insistent, low, authoritative voice punctuated by slightly higher tones for playful banter or for infrequent praise that usually was limited to a simple statement of "good" or "okay." Social distance was maintained between adults and children. The adults in center E also maintained a bit of aloofness from the children and used a polite but authoritative tone to emphasize instructions for behavior. Their commands, however, tended to be less stern than in center A. Center E personnel often praised children for a correct response to a command by enthusiastically saying "very good" or "right."

In center B, Miss Beth used a low authoritative tone only when she issued imperative commands to the children. During frequent playful and affectionate interactions, she used a very high tone sprinkled with "sweetie's" and "darlin's." Her speech was rapid and the tones seemed to be exaggerated, with very low tones expressing warning or displeasure and very high tones expressing affection or pleading for cooperation.

In center C, adult speech also tended to be within a fairly high tonal range and almost never authoritative. Sentences tended to be short, simple, and only slightly more complex than the child's own speech. Adults spoke softly. Their occasional reprimands were more soberly pleading than Miss Beth's and sometimes expressed mild dismay or disbelief. For example, when Cora saw one toddler pull another toddler's hair, she bent down, took the hair-puller's hands gently but with an intense look of sadness and concern, said, "Oh, no. Ouch! Pulling hair hurts. No pulling hair, please." Adults spoke to children at close range, face-to-face, often repeating short, simple speech sequences until the children gave some indication of comprehension. Instead of speaking in exaggerated low adult tones to intimidate cooperation, the staff members of center C adapted their voices to the range and inflection of the babies' voices and in response to indications of their attention. Bernstein [1971] has identified the tendency of parents in the person-oriented mode to adapt to, and be socialized by actions initiated by the child.

The focal point of control in center A was unilateral, unquestioning obedience appropriate to one's position as a child. Mrs. Aiken said, "They gotta know their place." The focus of control in center E was on gaining the cooperation of the children for teacher-directed activities in a way more genteel but somewhat similar to center A's focus on getting the children to obey. Center E valued group compliance for teacher-directed routines, where center A valued a more submissive form of obedience to authority. In center B, the focal point seemed to be on expediency, getting through each day with each individual baby as safe and content as possible. In center C, the focal point of control was on individual rights and personal development. The environment was designed to be free of unacceptable dangers, and the children were allowed to test their own skills with little intervention.

Curriculum Methodology

Perceptions of individual or categorical rationales for children's behavior fit generally with ideas of child-centered (personal) and teacher-centered (positional) teaching methodology. The center C staff saw children as inherently well-intentioned individuals with the capacity for inappropriate or misguided behavior. When Christina was asked what she would say or do if a toddler repeatedly knocked over a glass of milk, she said, "I would try and get an exercise in my classroom that would satisfy their need for dumping"—an indication that she would follow the child's lead in creating curriculum content. Miss Beth often chose or avoided specific toys or games for individual children whom she claimed "loved" puzzles or "hated" to play "pat-a-cake."

In contrast, in center A, Mrs. Aiken talked of "breaking" newly enrolled babies. When toddlers lost interest in long recitation exercises, she generalized, "They don't seem like they have the initiative to want to go on and try to say the alphabets"—an indication of her commitment to an adult-selected curriculum agenda. In center E, after a group of one-year-olds had sat for 20 minutes of teacher-directed activity with flash-cards and geometric coloring sheets, a teacher explained the whining and misbehavior of several children by saying, "This group is tired. I've worked them pretty hard this morning."

The teaching methods of centers A and E, on one hand, would clearly be defined as teacher, or curriculum, centered. Knowledge was perceived by adults to be a body of information given to the children as a group. Children were assumed to need certain types of knowledge and skill based on their position as children of a certain age. Centers B and C, on the other hand, subscribed to a child-centered methodology—learning was perceived by these adults to be an internal developmental process carried out by the child and facilitated or hindered by the adult. Differences in the child-centered and teacher-centered methods are clearly indicated also by the fact that center C, and to a lesser extent Center B, made available elaborately differentiated and organized materials designed for spontaneous child-directed learning activity. Centers A and E, however, grouped objects into two categories, toys for child-initiated but trivial entertainment (available on a limited basis), and generally more abstract materials for teacher-directed learning activity that was perceived to be the significant curriculum component.

Differences among the centers are further highlighted by the differences between centers A and C in their attitudes about sleeping in class. While Mrs. Aiken's one- and two-year-old children were sitting in chairs for two or more hours, as was their usual morning routine, they predictably began falling asleep. Sleeping seemed to be the preferred method of resisting Mrs. Aiken's teaching, since passive resistance was tolerated, and active resistance, such as getting up off the chairs, consistently resulted in immediate and firm reprimand. During one particularly long morning, Mrs. Aiken looked up from the book, about a black hole in the universe, that she was reading and noticed that four of her seven students were asleep. Instead of perceiving that the book was inappropriate or uninteresting to the children, she perceived that the children were being uncooperative. She said:

> Wake up, Arthur. Wake up, Arthur. I said wake up! That was a good story, wasn't it. I liked that one. All of you wake up! I'm going to have to wake you all up, ain't I. Hmmm. M'gonna havta wake you up. Annie's tryin' to go to sleep on me. Andy's tryin' to go to sleep on me. Audrey's tryin' to go to sleep on me. Annie, stand up for a while. Walk around and try to wake up. Don't fall down.

In center C, a child rubbing his eyes was immediately asked if he wanted to lie down. When he indicated that he did, a mat was put down for him and he was gently helped to lie down. At the normal nap time, he was given books and puzzles to play with while the other children slept.

Centers A and E demonstrated, through their teacher-centered methods, a positional orientation, in that the adult's role as teacher authorizes the adult to decide what the child will learn. In centers B and C, the child-centered methodology indicates a personal orientation in that learning must be related to an individual child's interests and abilities and must not be imposed externally.

Additionally, center C demonstrated alliance with an interactionist philosophical perspective in which learning is thought to be the result of the interaction between exposure to a challenging environment and the internal maturation and production of the child. Center A assumed a kind of traditionalist position in viewing the teacher as the external provider of knowledge but also in viewing the child as having power over what he or she will actively choose to learn. Center B demonstrated alliance with a maturationist philosophical perspective in which learning is perceived to result from normal growth and development within a reasonably supportive environment. Center E demonstrated philosophical alliance with behaviorist philosophy, in which learning is perceived to be a result of externally controlled teaching.

Hierarchical and Egalitarian Role Relationships

Role relationships among adults in each of the centers also reflected the personal or positional orientation evident in each setting. In center A, where the mode of controlling children was positional, the social relationship of the adults to each other was also positional, or hierarchical. Administrators used a positional mode for controlling or managing staff members. Mrs. Aiken routinely asked permission of the director before making even minor changes or decisions. In center E, a clear hierarchy also existed in which assistants were assigned menial chores such as feeding and diapering, and teachers were assigned more prestigious chores based on their positions.

In center C, where children were socialized in a relatively egalitarian fashion by flexible, even compliant adults, the adults were person-oriented in their administrative dealings with each other. Communication was open and the division of labor was flexible, based not only on job roles and responsibilities but also on personal ability and availability. The director was as quick as any other staff member to change a diaper or wipe a spill if it needed to be done and she was available. Staff members had a remarkable level of input into administrative policy and curriculum decisions. In center B, the director accepted Miss Beth's style of caring for the babies even though it was not in total compliance with written procedures. She acknowledged Miss Beth's personal interests and preferences just as Miss Beth adapted to individual children's interests and preferences. In centers B and C an informal intimacy and camaraderie existed among coworkers who hugged, laughed, teased, and complained with each other and the director. This contrasted with the more formal deference maintained between caregivers and administrators in centers A and E.

The social role relationships between adults and children seemed to be an extension of the hierarchical or egalitarian patterns of interaction between administration and staff. In center A, the children were addressed formally as a group, "Good morning, children," with children responding in unison, "Good morning, Mrs. Anderson." Teachers often gave praise and reprimands to the entire group, for example, "You all have done very good this morning." On one rare occasion when Mrs. Aiken picked up and hugged a one-year-old, playfully praising her, the other toddlers snapped to full attention, startled by this unusual occurrence. Center E staff members were polite but restrained in their interactions with the children. Some staff members seemed not to know all of the children's names, and few toddlers were observed calling adults by any name other than teacher. The staff consistently referred, however, to parents as Mr. or Mrs. whenever a parent was addressed by name.

In center B, whenever Miss Betty gave individual praise, other children scrambled to be included in the attention. Miss Beth carried babies on her hip, playfully hoisted them in the air, and patted and rocked them. Several were heard calling her "mama." In center C, staff members and children were also warm and intimate in their interactions. One- and two-year-olds who could talk knew the names of and called teachers, directors, and even the owner by their first names. Praise and affection were liberally offered while reprimands were muted, private, and given sparingly. Praise was so routine that children seemed unconcerned about recognition received by other children.

Another interesting aspect of social role relations in the centers was the nomenclature used by the staff of each center. The first day I visited Alphabet Academy, I said that my name was Darla Miller. I was asked if I was a "Miss" or a "Mrs.," then I was introduced to the children as Mrs. Miller. The staff never referred to me or to each other by first names. Remarkably, in an all black, low-income center visited during preliminary screening, I asked a teacher the first name of her coworker. When she said that she did not know the woman's first name, I expressed surprise and said, "Oh, I thought you said you'd worked together for six years." She answered, "Yes, but she never told me her first name. She says if the children ever heard her first name, that's all they would call her." Obviously, in center A, one's formal or positional name was perceived to be more appropriate than one's informal or personal name. The younger children never attempted my name, but on the first day that I brought a tape recorder, a cluster of curious children gathered around me. Arlin, who was almost three, leaned close to me after watching my silent tape recorder for several minutes and said, "Lae, cu da uh." I didn't understand him, but a five-year-old told me that Arlin said, "Hey, lady, cut that thing up." On another occasion, two kindergarten-aged children asked me if I had brought their new paint brushes. When I said no, one responded, "It musta' been that other white lady." In center A, I was categorized as a "white lady" while in the other three predominantly white centers, I was occasionally called "teacher" by older children.

When I first visited Balloons and Bunnies Learning Center and gave my first and last names to the director, she took me back to the nursery and introduced me as Miss Darla. The staff usually, but not always, referred to each other in that manner. Miss Beth never remembered my name though, so on occasion she referred to me as "Miss, uh, Miss Little Sweet Pies." Her lack of formality was also evidenced at the end of my second observation of her class when, as I prepared to leave, she put her arms around me, saying, "I think I'll give you a hug." As has previously been noted, Miss Beth seemed to talk to the babies as if she were thinking out loud rather than expecting them to understand her. She carried on one monologue, and the babies, with their Spartan one-word sentences that often lacked beginning and ending consonants, carried on another. I especially noticed that the one-year-olds frequently said mama when they wanted Miss Beth's attention, but that she seemed not to really notice. One day I asked her what she wanted the children to call her. She looked at me with a blank stare and said, "They don't call me nothin'. They cain't talk." The use of "Miss" with first names was assumed to indicate a polite but informal role relationship.

On my first visit to the cottage of Color-Coordinated Country Day School, I was greeted by Cora and Chelsey. Cora said, "Chelsey, let's take Darla out on the deck and introduce her to everyone." A two-year-old child sitting on the potty who heard us peeked out and said with a shy grin, "Where Dardo [Darla]?" Several other toddlers nearby said, "Hewo [hello] Dardo. Bye, bye, Dardo," and giggled. On the deck, Chelsey pointed at each child and slowly and deliberately said, "Ko-wee [Cory]. Cha-woh [Charles]. Hempia [Cynthia]. Cowah [Cora]." Chelsey then looked at me and continued several more times around the group, waiting after each name for me to nod acknowledgment. The use of names in center C indicated an almost peer-type relationship between the adults and the children in which nomenclature was not used to designate position but rather to emphasize the equalitarian status of child and adult roles.

In center E, adults spoke to each other in an informal manner using first names. As in center B, however, the use of names was somewhat aloof from the children. Adults called both other adults and children by their first names, but no children were observed (during the very limited observations made of center E) calling adults by any name. Toddlers were heard saying "Teetow [teacher]" to get adult attention. The staff, interestingly, referred to parents as Mr. and Mrs., indicating perhaps that in this hierarchical setting the parents occupied a social niche that was perceived to be a rung higher than that held by the child care workers.

A final note about social role relations is the use or nonuse of what often is termed baby talk. In center A, the adults maintained a teacherly tone, a manner of speaking that would seem equally appropriate in a sixth grade arithmetic class. The teachers spoke to children in an insistent, authoritative voice punctuated by higher tones for playful banter or for infrequent praise that usually was limited to a simple statement of "good" or "okay." Affection was expressed in lyrical mock reprimand. For example, "You a bad, bad, bad, lady today, ain't you. Yes you is. I know you is. Gimme some sugar, you bad lady."

In center B, Miss Beth used a low authoritative tone much of the time as she issued imperative commands to the children. On playful and affectionate occasions, she used a very high tone sprinkled with "sweetie's" and "darlin's." Her speech was rapid, and although the words were generally like that used with other adults, the tones seemed to be exaggerated, with very low tones expressing warning or displeasure and very high tones expressing pleasure and affection. Miss Betty and Miss Bonnie used more mid-tones and fewer very high or very low tones. Their reprimands often were in a fairly high, pleading rather than demanding tone, and their expressions of affection tended to be slightly lower than reprimands. On some occasions they did use a low, firm, authoritative tone to express displeasure with a child's behavior. Their tonal range seemed somewhat subdued, however, compared to Miss Beth's openly expressive range.

In center C, adult speech also tended to be lyrical and almost constantly within a fairly high tonal range. Sentences tended to be very short and simple, only slightly more complex than the child's own speech. Adults almost always spoke softly; their speech was often almost impossible to understand on my tape recordings, even when the recorder was turned to full volume. Their occasional reprimands were softly pleading and sometimes conveyed disappointment or disbelief.

Adults often punctuated bright, conversational banter with little gasps. For example, "Would you like to go outside? (little gasp) You would!" They liberally used exaggerated facial expressions and hand and body gestures to convey meaning. And they regularly repeated a word or a name very slowly dropping from a higher to a lower tone. This slow, musical dropping in tone, although a frequent feature of center C, was rarely heard at B, and never observed at centers A and E. In music literature [Zimmerman 1971; High 1985] this tonal dropping is called the falling third, and is termed the most natural interval for children to sing and the most frequently child-initiated musical combination. Even a baby's cry drops from high to low.

Center C's use of the falling third in verbal interaction is indicative of the staff's overall adaptation to the child. Instead of speaking in very low tones to intimidate cooperation or in very high tones to catch attention, the staff members of center C routinely modulated their voices to the range and inflection of the babies. Bernstein [1971] has identified the tendency of parents in the person-oriented mode to adapt to and be socialized by actions initiated by the child. Tonal ranges in center E, although not fully explored, seemed to be somewhat similar to those used in center B.

Gender Differentiation

Another feature of the social structures in the centers related to male and female roles. In center A, boys were usually seated on one side of a long table and girls on the other side, with the girls almost always positioned closer to the teacher. Mrs. Aiken said that the girls were "more spoilder" and "more friskier" than the boys, "they like a lotsa attention, more so than the boys...they mamas tend to spoil 'em more, you know."

In center A, girls were more firmly and more frequently reprimanded than boys. Boys were more likely to pout and girls more likely to take action to resolve conflicts. When Arlin picked up Annie's barrette and tried to put it in his hair, Mrs. Aiken sternly told him that barrettes were for girls. Mrs. Aiken's toddlers were absorbing gender stereotypes even before they understood their own sexual identity. When Annie tried to put the barrette back in her hair, Arlin also told her to leave the barrette alone, "That for girls!" Male and female roles reflected a positional orientation based on gender, and children clearly were expected to learn sex-appropriate behaviors.

In center B, Miss Betty often seated her two-year-old boys at the end of the table with other boys, but her differences in treatment of boys and girls were very subtle. She praised girls more often and showed more tolerance toward them than toward the boys. Miss Beth had only boys in her group, but she persisted in calling the younger ones "she" or "her." When she spoke tenderly to the children she was more likely to use feminine pronouns, and when she reprimanded or spoke of older, bigger children, she was more likely to use masculine pronouns. Bernstein [1979] states that persons in the restricted/personal orientation tend to view individuals in terms of their generally assumed characteristics rather than in terms of their unique characteristics.

"Little bitty" babies seemed to be viewed as generically feminine to Miss Beth. Additionally, Miss Beth said that girls were born different from boys, and that infant girls only cried if they were hungry or tired but that boy infants would cry for no reason. Her gender-based discrimination was not geared to teaching acceptable sex roles but rather an acknowledgment of perceived inherent differences. In center C, there was a minimum of differentiation between girls and boys. Boys were encouraged to play with dolls and girls were encouraged to be assertive. In center E, some degree of gender-role expectation was evidenced and there were differences in the regulation of behavior, but differentiation between girls and boys was considerably less than in centers A and B.

Summary

Caregivers in the centers clearly gave evidence of differing perceptions of the needs of babies. In centers A and E, crying was not necessarily perceived to indicate a need. In centers B and C, crying was almost always perceived to indicate need. In center A, Mrs. Aiken described a newly admitted baby who cried for days, "She didn't need nothin', she just wanted her mama." Bottles and pacifiers were not allowed in center A since "they are a lot of trouble to worry with and the babies don't really need them anyway. They holler for a few days and then they forget about them." In center A, crying was dealt with as a kind of misbehavior that sometimes warranted punishment.

In center B, crying was perceived as a possible indication of need, even, perhaps, an indication of adult negligence. Whenever several babies started to cry at the same time, Miss Beth said that they were either hungry or tired. When a baby fell and bumped his head, Miss Beth said, "He ain't hurt, he's just yelling 'cause he's mad." However, when I asked Miss Beth what she thought several screaming one-year-olds needed, she defensively answered, "They don't need nothin', they're happy all the time." Miss Beth did not punish crying, but she was most emphatic in her pleas and demands that babies stop crying.

Personnel in center C allowed themselves to be at the mercy of the babies. A baby's cry was always perceived to be a clear indication of some kind of need and the adults were held responsible to find a solution. Caregivers were expected to use trial and error methods for finding a way to solve the child's problem, whatever it was. If nothing worked and crying persisted over a period of hours, parents were telephoned and the responsibility of finding a solution was shifted to them. Staff members were quick to acknowledge needs. With heavy sighs they said that the babies needed more individual attention, and the adults needed more time to meet individual needs. Cora said, "Oh, they just need so much and there is never enough time."

In center E, crying seemed to be perceived as a simple annoyance typical of babies, to be avoided if at all possible, but of no particular consequence in terms of the child's real needs. A teacher who repeatedly insisted that a seven-month-old not put a toy in her mouth was unmoved when the baby finally slumped onto the floor crying. Interestingly, the most crying was heard in centers B and E, possibly because adults responded to crying in a rather unpredictable manner, sometimes indulging, sometimes ignoring. Center A had almost no crying, probably because crying was dealt with in a predictable and consistent manner and never indulged. (Adults responded according to their own perceived notions of right and wrong, not as a response to crying.) Center C was consistent in responding immediately and flexibly to comfort and assist a crying child. Crying was allowed and sympathy was expressed.

The manner in which each of the settings is defined may be seen as an interpretation by caregivers of the world as they see it. If caregivers expect a gentle compliant world that is permeable and responsive, that is the kind of world that is created for the young child. If the world is perceived to be cold, hard, and unbending, then children are plunged into it just as some primitive cultures plunged their infants into ice water to toughen them for survival. Calling children epithets, pointing out their failures, and denying indulgences are ways of habituating and thus protecting them from future hurts and disappointments, avoiding false expectations of ease and comfort. Indulging and pampering prepare children for a very different existence.

A child socialized to existence in a setting of poverty and inequality may have low expectations and low self-esteem but highly effective coping skills. The street-wise working-class infants in this study knew better than to touch the grating propped precariously in front of the electric heater or to roll off the diapering table when their teacher left the room. Naive, protected middle-class children would surely be unprepared for daily hazards the low-income children handled with ease. Children socialized to a life of privilege may be confident, verbal, and creative, but they may join the epidemic of adolescent suicides when the real world proves colder and harder than expected.

Socialization to a permeable, flexible world fits into Bernstein's definition of socialization to an elaborated code. Socialization to a rigid, impermeable world fits into his definition of socialization to a restricted code. Early differential enculturation clearly makes sense in terms of its adapting children to specific cultural settings. Differential enculturation, however, is problematic for a democratic society. Successful adaptation to one set of circumstances will tend to limit one's effectiveness to that setting, since learned patterns of behavior that are expected in one situation may be viewed as nonfunctional and inappropriate in other settings.

VII

CONCLUSION

Through ethnographic description and qualitative analysis, this study argues that by age three, significant enculturation through the absorption of linguistic code and social role expectations has already taken place. The arrow has left the bow, and while its final destination is not assured, it has begun a given course through the air. Day care centers must not be viewed as providing kindly custodial care only for society members who are too immature to participate in social processes, but rather as crucially important cultural settings that bend fragile twigs and leave a mark on the great oak trees of future generations.

The present study has set about to identify and examine infant/toddler day care centers that were considered to be of high quality by their clientele and community. If quantitative studies had been undertaken to compare and contrast the four centers, the centers might have appeared to be deceptively similar, especially if one had controlled for differences based on financial resources alone. All four centers were bright and clean. (One could smell the fresh pine scent of disinfectant cleaner from outside the front door of center A, and soiled diapers were individually wrapped before disposal in center E.) All four staffs evidenced their commitment to and concern for the children. And all four centers had specific curricular goals and strategies. None of the four centers studied represented the segment of day care that is pathological or that deprives and neglects children.

Even the self-reporting of routines by members of the four

staffs was surprisingly similar. Mrs. Aiken, from a low socioeconomic day care setting, and Cora, from a very high one, both
reported that they would have toddlers "clean up" milk that was
spilled. The subtle magic of qualitative methodology is that the
researcher can learn that Mrs. Aiken would "make" them clean it
and Cora would "invite" them to clean it. This slight difference in
semantics delineates differences in teacher-child role relationship
expectations between Mrs. Aiken and Cora.

Adult caregivers in the centers tended to represent class fractions somewhat different from the families they served, and a range
of socioeconomic backgrounds existed within individual centers
from the directors down to the aides. There was, however, a
consistency of code and control in each center that matched fairly
closely the linguistic codes and modes of control to be expected in
the class fractions of the client families. Although parent behavior
was not a key focus of this study, participant observation provided
serendipitous indications that clients did indeed use and expect
caregivers to use the codes and modes of control seen in the centers.
Also, one staff member, an aide, was observed using a mode of
control with her own toddler outside the center that matched her
socioeconomic background but not that of the affluent center in
which she worked. Interestingly, her control methods in the center
were consistent with the prevailing methods seen there.

In center C, the center with affluent, highly educated,
professional/managerial parents, which has been described as
evidencing person-oriented control and elaborated linguistic code,
there was a very high level of give-and-take among children and
caregivers. Children actively engaged in negotiating with authority
figures and freely accommodated or resisted gentle pressures of the
adults to socialize them. Adults seemed to interpret mild resistance
as a positive indication of the child's growing autonomy. They
viewed overt resistance either as an indication that their own
expectations were unwarranted or that the child was suffering
underlying adjustment problems stemming from not having
primary needs properly met.

Children generally cooperated with the adults since the
children's use of time, space, and objects in the center depended
almost exclusively on daily choices or preferences indicated by the
infants and toddlers themselves. The children were treated with
respect by caregivers. The rights, comforts, and interests of the
individual child were at the focal point of curriculum decisions. All
learning goals were couched in terms of individual development
and fulfillment—with the achievement of responsible independence the highest goal. These infants and toddlers were clearly being

prepared for the social milieu of their privileged parents, who were primarily employed in creative, self-directed, and highly respected occupations.

In center E, the center serving primarily business executive elite parents, which has been described as evidencing position-oriented control and elaborated linguistic code, there was a pervasive sense that babies were pampered and highly valued products. The degree of measurable performance by children in academic tasks was the focal point of curriculum decisions. Children were positively reinforced for absorbing as much memorized information as they could reasonably handle via abstract symbols for quantities, letters, and geometric shapes. They were allowed to depend on the authority figures for care, and the hierarchy of authority figures made decisions controlling most of the use of space, time, and objects.

Adults were not amused by nor particularly tolerant of resistance by babies to adult agendas. Resisting children were at first ignored and, if persistent, firmly redirected. Compliance, receptivity, and attentiveness were valued by caregivers, but high-quality performance was clearly at the heart of learning goals. Many of the children's parents were powerful members of society who compete in the highly positional "good ol' boy" system in which compliance, being a "company" man or woman, and the ability to perform on cue help one rise through the hierarchy of power and financial remuneration. The business executive parents in this center generally had lower levels of education and similar or, in some cases, higher levels of income when compared to the professional parents from center C, but it must be remembered that although doctors, lawyers, and professors can have the capacity to influence political and economic power, business executives may be that power.

In center B, the middle socioeconomic center, which has been identified as evidencing person-oriented control and restricted linguistic code, children were engaged in a tug-of-war with caregivers, alternately socializing and being socialized. Children were expected to depend on caregivers, they were expected to compete with peers for attention and toys (resources), and although they were allowed to make some demands on the authority figures, they were expected to tolerate their circumstances without too much stridence. They learned to accept occasional boredom and some intrusiveness by the authority figures. The children maintained a steady but innocuous level of resistance to authority figures. The adults seemed tolerant of, resigned to, and often amused by the babies' perceived "naughtiness."

Safety, avoidance of conflict, adherence to set routines, and maintenance of the status quo seemed to be the criteria for curriculum decisions. Learning goals for the children were focused on providing a nurturing environment so that normal development could take place. There was a sense that ultimate outcomes were somehow predetermined by fate. Many of these children's parents were middle-level supervisors in factories, small-business owners, and participants in other occupations in which one may be less able to control the circumstances surrounding one's work. One may be at the mercy of economic trends, the whims of superiors, or of bureaucracy in general. One's occupational success may depend on avoidance of conflict and adherence to set procedures in a setting where swimming against the tide may be useless or counterproductive.

In center A, the center with a semiskilled and unskilled working-class family clientele, which has been described as evidencing position-oriented control and restricted linguistic code, children were treated as underlings with few rights. The word of the teacher was law, to be obeyed without question—although high levels of resistance seemed expected. Resistance was sometimes arbitrarily punished, but, at other times, it seemed to delight or amuse caregivers. Conformity and group cohesion along with rote memorization were the basis for curriculum decisions. The children were not overprotected or directly controlled during rowdy physical play times. They had almost total freedom in this arena and were remarkably strong and agile, and had mastered many physical aspects of the environment.

Through play and work, these children learned to cope with environmental dangers, long periods of crushing boredom, and the lack of plentiful material resources. They learned to care for the physical needs of one another, to suppress impulses, to tolerate discomfort, and to passively resist authority. One staff member said, "Nobody likes somebody who's too perfect. You want 'em to be a little bit bad."

The Center A children became habituated, and thus impervious, to criticism and punishment, and developed subtle methods to appear compliant while secretively resisting authority. They also learned to channel creative and expressive urges into group singing, dancing, and playing. These activities were uninhibited, powerful, and charged with social energy. Academic work was passive and plodding. The parents of these children almost all did menial and repetitive work. They were clearly at the mercy of forces outside their grasp. Their economic security probably depended on physical strength and skill, an appearance of obedience, a support system among kin, and conformity to set routines. Their self-esteem probably depended on a tough resistance to insult and on community outlets for pleasure and self-expression. The socialization strategies used by caregivers made perfect sense in terms of the realities of life experiences. However, those skills and behaviors that are functional in one cultural setting also undoubtedly conflict with expectations in other settings and hamper mobility from one cultural setting to another.

Each of the center directors observed during this study indicated a remarkable commitment to her belief system for the care and education of very young children. None of the four had passively accepted the ideologies and roles set forth in the centers. Each director was passionate about the rightness of her method and starkly critical of other methods. Black and Hispanic assistants accepted and carried out the role expected of them in center C, although at least one used methods more similar to center A with her own toddler and infant on her own time.

Discussion with the group of experts on black culture (described in the methods section) uncovered resentment toward governmental policy makers for imposing middle-class, child-centered methods on low-income day care centers. They argued that such methods were "an import from the white community" and unrelated to the "special" needs of black children. Interestingly, however, almost all of the successful black professionals in that group had sought out distinctly child-centered day care settings for their own children although they expressed a great deal of inner conflict about that decision. One highly successful black professor and mother of three, whose daughter had encountered flexibility in her child-centered day care center and now pressured her parents for flexibility, said, "I know I should be more flexible but I keep thinking, 'What would my mother say?'" Social change brings stress, but the most expedient and powerful tool for intervention into early childhood socialization is probably the restructuring of the daily working and living conditions of parents and caregivers. There seems to be some powerful urge in human beings to replicate for children the social reality they perceive from their own experience in the larger society.

Theoretical Implications

The study of very early socialization is an almost overwhelmingly complex undertaking, but it holds the promise of a greater understanding of human behavior. Subtle cultural differences that almost seem innate can be traced to clearly differentiated roots. Infancy, the period from birth to three, has often been dismissed by educators and sociologists as a custodial period of physiological maturation. Parents and teachers have said, "First children must learn to walk, talk, and use the toilet, then we can begin the important process of socialization and education." Only recently has there emerged a growing awareness of the invisible curriculum that shapes earliest perceptions of self and society.

As Piaget and others have demonstrated in their studies of the earliest stages of human development—intellectual and creative giftedness is a dynamic, reciprocal interaction between a child and his or her environment. Genius is not a condition but rather the continuous process of adaptation and accommodation carried out by a subject in a situation. This process develops so slowly, day by day from the time prenatal sensory perception is intact, that to a casual observer a child's character and competence may seem wholly innate.

Through ethnographic description and qualitative analysis, this study argues that by age three, significant enculturation through the absorption of linguistic code and social role expectations has already taken place. Day care centers must be viewed as crucially important cultural settings that bend fragile twigs and leave their mark on the great oak trees of future generations.

In this country, day care is generally considered an educationally insignificant personal matter for families. Also, there is virtually no coherent or comprehensive public funding or policy making that deals with early day care. Consequently, there may be more differential socialization presently occurring in this area, and more potential for intervention into patterns of enculturation that tend to stabilize economic inequality within social strata, than from any other area of education. Day care is the bridge between parenting and formal educational institutions, and the period from birth to three years of age is the bridge from that which is organically a human being to that which is specifically and culturally a social being.

Social reproduction theorists argue that economically, politically, and socially stratified societies produce, through one mechanism or another, educational structures that reproduce similar stratification [Bowles and Gintis 1976; Willis 1981; Apple 1982; Giroux 1981; Bourdieu and Passeron 1977]. This view has been criticized as overly deterministic, and emphasis on the impact of resistance and accommodation as part of the socialization process has been considered [Anyon 1981]. Berlak and Berlak [1981] argue that the socialization process is dialectical, that individuals, although limited and conditioned by the social environment, have the power to alter the social conditions around them.

In the present study, adult caregivers indicated a fairly high level of conscious intention in their development of child care ideologies. Mrs. Anderson resisted an ideology of child-centered care that she was required to learn as part of her university study. She said that it was "just wrong." Miss Beth resisted pressure from her director to follow a daily lesson plan, and happily described her role as "just a playin' and a changin'." Directors and teachers in centers C and E discussed strategies for "parent education," to share with parents the ideologies and methods used in the centers. The directors and teachers observed in the course of this study seemed more like crusaders for their various ideologies than "mere objects shaped by economic forces and structures" [Berlak and Berlak 1981]. Their beliefs about the rightness or wrongness of child care strategies and role relationships seemed to derive from the history and tradition of their own social contexts as well as from their present perceptions of the social world. Their adoption of various folk ideologies seemed to be solidified by tradition and social history but made fluid by perceptions and interpretations of day-to-day reality. Caregivers in the centers were in a continuing process of accommodation and resistance to socialization from the external social world of universities, parents, and other influences, as well as from the infants and toddlers in care.

In contrast, the accommodation and resistance to socialization seen in the infants and toddlers indicated the physical and developmental laws of nature more than any conscious interpretation of meaning. Center A children fell asleep during long stories because sleep was an escape from the discomfort and stress of long periods sitting still on chairs. Center C children negotiated with adult caregivers because they had become conditioned to expect compliant adults. Adults unwittingly contributed to the development of accommodation and resistance styles in children by variously punishing, reinforcing, or ignoring active and passive acts of resistance. Children in each of the centers had typical and predictable styles of resistance to socialization. Center A children hurried to retrieve and eat a sack of candy from the teacher's table while she was out of the room; center B children cried until they were given the crackers they wanted before lunch; center C children resisted assertively through verbal and nonverbal indications of their preferences; and center E children stubbornly looked away from flash cards placed in front of their faces.

Adult expectations and perceptions were transmitted to children in subtle ways. A black caregiver described little boys as "the clay that resists molding," a view that parallels Anyon's [1981] assertion that working-class students may resist schooling because they believe that it is too much work for too little chance of success. Although the infants and toddlers in this study were too young to contemplate such global cause-and-effect considerations, they were not too young to be shaped by caregivers' general perceptions of motives as expressed in day-to-day interactions and responses to various behaviors. Adult behaviors based on folk ideologies, and infant/toddler behaviors based on physiological laws of development interact in a dialectical manner, influencing and influenced by the hegemony of a given social context and ultimately contributing to the reproduction of social strata. This study has followed in the theoretical tradition of social reproduction research and has documented through qualitative methodology various factors that contribute, as early as the first year of life, to the socialization of children into socioeconomic strata.

Methodological Implications

This preliminary description of socialization outside the home of children from birth to three years of age has attempted to define folk ideologies that may be typical of various levels of socioeconomic strata and that may unwittingly contribute to structures of social inequity. Ethnographic description based on participant observation, in-depth interviews, still photography, and audiotape recording has been subjected to domain and taxonomic analysis and has resulted in a set of propositions related to the differential socialization of very young children by child care workers.

A field-intensive strategy for the study of infant/toddler day care has been especially helpful, since a limited body of pertinent literature was available, and this research has necessarily been exploratory in nature. Participant observation made it possible to step into the shoes of various caregivers and to get a sense of the day-to-day experiences of very young children in day care. By attempting to model the participant observer's actions in the centers after the behaviors of the child care workers there, the field researcher began to recognize subjective ideological perspectives more clearly and to understand the rationales for ideological perspectives in the centers.

Audiotape recording of daily events as well as of structured interviews was also advantageous in making it possible to retrieve details of various events during the transcription of field notes or the process of analysis. By listening to tapes many times, the field researcher became aware of overall rhythms and qualities of tones in the various centers that contributed to an understanding of the events in them. Photographs taken on the last day of observation in each center were especially helpful for examining details of body language, facial expression, posture, and position that were missed during the busy flow of events in the centers.

A key area for methodological redesign of a future study of this type would be the provision of additional data from parents. Although visits to the homes of the children, or part of the children, would be time consuming, it would be valuable in identifying more clearly the similarities and differences in child care styles among caregivers and parents. Data from the present study could also be used as a basis for future quantitative research that could confirm or refute the representativeness of the lists of characteristics identified as part of various folk ideologies.

Implications for Policy and Practice

A great deal of effort and expense has been channeled by policy makers and educators into caregiver training that may have imposed middle-class child care ideologies onto low-income caregivers. There should be little wonder that methods conflicting with cultural ideologies of working-class groups have been resented and resisted. Knowledge of cultural differences may increase sensitivity and bring about policies that increase economic mobility for individual children without trampling the cultural values of adults who care for them. No educational policy can be effective if it has nothing to do with anything real for those expected to live and work within its guidelines.

Anyon [1981] documents the tendency in public elementary schools for teachers to assume that working-class children are "lazy" and to perceive that what they need is simplistic, mechanical, rote memorization. That view implies an unresponsive school system that is not sensitive to and does not meet the needs of working-class children. This study describes child care workers at the infant/toddler level selected by and paid privately by parents, who say that a one-year-old who does not say the alphabet may not have the "initiative to want to do it," and who champion the use of simplistic, mechanical rote memorization. Future study is needed to determine how much of that behavior is accepted, even expected, by parents simply because it has been lived (and is a result of school experiences), and how much of it exists as part of a self-fulfilling prophesy through which children socialize their teachers and change teacher expectations for specific groups of children. The results of this study would indicate that such a process is dialectical and therefore would include influences from both teachers and children.

Another area of professional concern that has resulted from this study is the widespread endorsement of one ideology of child care that may be found in much of the academic literature that is focused on how to provide quality care for young children. Textbooks and practice journals often subscribe openly to the child-centered methods of center C with the assumption that quality care must be flexible and based on individual interests and abilities. Academic alliance with the ideologies of center C seems plausible, since the writers of journals and textbooks might be expected to occupy a level of socioeconomic status similar to the professionals of center C.

Professional perceptions of alternate ideologies as nonquality child care have probably hindered many publicly funded programs aimed at individual socioeconomic mobility. Based on the findings of this study, intervention programs must not be aimed at changing individual children in spite of their presenting cultures, but instead must focus on helping caregivers and child care planners think through the long-term implications of various child care ideologies, and on helping them consequently develop ideologies that they perceive to make sense and to be functional and compatible with cultural values.

Lubeck [1985], in her ethnographic study of early childhood education in preschool and Headstart, asserts that caregivers are not helpless pawns in a system but active constructors of a meaningful and consistent order that works within, and even in opposition to, the constraints of the bureaucratic order of their supervisors and society at large.

The socialization of young children in day care does not take place in a social vacuum. It is part of a dynamic dialectical process in which effects ripple downward from social and economic structures to child care workers to children, and upward from children to workers and back to larger institutions. Institutions, caregivers, and children constantly change and are changed by the process. However, when one steps back to look at the big picture, the dynamic rippling changes become part of the overall stability, like continuing adjustments of a balance pole by a tight-rope walker. The macrolevel structures of resource inequity inch along with surprising consistency in spite of, or because of, never-ending ripples of give-and-take that reach the microlevel and echo back.

Individual members of society are not pawns in a chess game but neither are they totally able to orchestrate and control their own destinies. Infants, toddlers, caregivers, and other members of society adopt strategies for day-to-day living based on what works and what seems to make sense in terms of their own personal experiences. Only changes in the self-conscious understanding of internal and external social systems and changes in day-to-day experiences cause individuals to seek and ultimately to accept real changes in social patterns.

REFERENCES

Adlam, D. *Code in Context*. London: Routledge and Kegan Paul, 1977.

Anyon, J. "Social Class and School Knowledge." *Curriculum Inquiry* 11, 1 (1981): 3–42.

———. "Intersections of Gender and Class: Accommodation and Resistance by Contradictory Sex-Role Ideologies." In *Gender, Class and Education*, edited by S. Walker and L. Barton. London: Falmer, 1983, pp. 21–37.

Apple, M. "Analyzing Determinations: Understanding and Evaluating the Production of Social Outcomes in Schools." *Curriculum Inquiry* 10 (Spring 1980): 55–76.

———. *Cultural and Economic Reproduction in Education: Essays on Class, Ideology and the State*. London: Routledge and Kegan Paul, 1982.

Aries, P. *Centuries of Childhood*. New York: Random House, 1962.

Belsky, J., and Steinberg, L.D. "The Effects of Day Care: A Critical Review." *Child Development* 49 (1978): 929–949.

Berlak, A., and Berlak, H. *Dilemmas of Schooling: Teaching and Social Change*. London: Methuen, 1981.

Bernstein, B. *Class, Codes and Control, Vol. 1. Theoretical Studies Toward a Sociology of Language*. London: Routledge and Kegan Paul, 1971.

———. "Family Role Systems, Socialization and Communication." In *Directions in Sociolinguistics*, edited by D. Hymes and J.J. Gumperz. New York: Holt, Rinehart and Winston, 1972.

———, ed. *Class, Codes and Control, Vol. 2. Applied Studies Towards a Sociology of Language*. London: Routledge and Kegan Paul, 1973.

———. "Sociology and the Sociology of Education: A Brief Account." In *Approaches to Sociology*, edited by J. Rex. London: Routledge and Kegan Paul, 1974.

———. *Class, Codes and Control, Vol. 3. Towards a Theory of Educational Transmissions*. London: Routledge and Kegan Paul, 1975.

———. "Social Class, Language and Socialization." In *Power and Ideology in Education*, edited by J. Karabel and A. H. Halsey. New York: Oxford University Press, 1979.

Bloom, L. "Language Development." In *Review of Child Development Research, Vol. 4*, edited by F. Horowitz. Chicago, IL: University of Chicago Press, 1973.

Bogdan, R., and Biklen, S.K. *Qualitative Research for Education: An Introduction to Theory and Methods*. Boston, MA: Allyn and Bacon, 1982.

Bourdieu, P., and Passeron, J. *La Reproduction*. Paris: Les Editions de Minuit, 1970.

———, and ———. *Reproduction in Education, Society and Culture*. Beverly Hills, CA: Sage, 1977.

Bowlby, J. *Attachment and Loss, Vol. 1*. New York: Basic Books, 1969.

Bowles, S. "Unequal Education and the Reproduction of the Social Division of Labor." *Review of Radical Political Economics* 3 (1971).

Bowles, S., and Gintis, H. "I. Q. in the U. S. Class Structure." *Social Policy* 3 (1972): 65–69.

———, and ———. *Schooling in Capitalist America*. London: Routledge and Kegan Paul, 1976.

Brandis, W., and Henderson, D. *Language, Primary Socialisation and Education, Vol. 1*, edited by B. Bernstein. London: Routledge and Kegan Paul, 1970.

Bremner, R. H. , ed. *Children and Youth in America: A Documentary History, Vols. 1–3*. Cambridge, MA: Harvard University Press, 1970–1974.

Children's Defense Fund. *A Children's Defense Budget: An Analysis of the FY 1987 Budget and Children*. Washington, DC: Children's Defense Fund, 1986.

Chomsky, N. *Aspects of the Theory of Syntax*. Cambridge, MA: M.I.T. Press, 1965.

Cicourel, A. V. *Language Use and School Performance*. New York: Academic Press, 1964.

Clark, B.R. *Educating the Expert Society*. San Francisco: Chandler, 1962.

Clarke-Stewart, A. "Popular Primers for Parents." *American Psychologist* 33 (1978): 359.

Cole, L. *A History of Education*. New York: Rinehart and Co., 1950.

Collins, R. "Functional Conflict Theories of Educational Stratification." *American Sociological Review* 36 (1971): 1002–1019.

Cook, J. A. "Language and Socialization." In *Class Codes and Control, Vol. 2. Applied Studies Towards a Sociology of Language*, edited by B. Bernstein. London: Routledge and Kegan Paul, 1973.

Cook-Gumperz, J. *Social Control and Socialization*. London: Routledge and Kegan Paul, 1979.

Dennis, W. *Children of the Creche*. New York: Appleton-Century-Crofts, 1973.

Durkheim, E. *L'Evolution Pedagogique en France*. Paris: Alcan, 1938.

Erikson, E.H. *Childhood and Society*. New York: Norton, 1950.

Fishman, J.A. "A Systematization of the Whorfian Hypothesis." *Behavioral Science* 5, University of Michigan Publication (1960).

———. "Who Speaks What Language to Whom and When?" *Linguistique* 2 (1965): 67–88.

Florio, S.E. *"Learning How to Go to School: An Ethnography of Interaction in a Kindergarten/First Grade Classroom."* Ph.D. diss., Harvard University: University Microfilms International (No. 7823676), 1985.

Froebel, F. *The Education of Man: The Art of Education, Instruction and Training*. New York: D. Appleton and Co., 1887.

Garfinkel, H. *Studies in Ethnomethodology*. Englewook Cliffs, NJ: Prentice-Hall, 1967.

Gesell, A. *Infancy and Human Growth*. New York: MacMillan, 1928.

Giroux, H. *Ideology, Culture, and the Process of Schooling*. Philadelphia, PA: Temple University Press, 1981.

Glaser, B., and Strauss, A.L. *The Discovery of Grounded Theory: Strategies for Qualitative Research*. Chicago, IL: Aldine, 1967.

Glubok, S., ed. *Home and Child Life in Colonial Days*. New York: Macmillan Publishing Co., 1969.

Halliday, M. *Explorations in the Function of Language*. London: Edward Arnold, 1973.

Harlow, H., and Zimmerman, R. "Affectional Responses in the Infant Monkey." *Science* 130 (1959): 421–432.

Hawkins, P. "Aspects of the Speech of Five-Year-Old Children." In *Class, Codes and Control*, edited by B. Bernstein. London: Routledge and Kegan Paul, 1973.

Henderson, D. "Contextual Specificity, Discretion, and Cognitive Socialisation: With Special Reference to Language." *Sociology* 4, 3 (1970).

Hess, E. "Imprinting in a Natural Laboratory." *Scientific American* 227 (1972): 24–31.

High, L. "Music for Young Children." Unpublished. Memphis, TN: 1985.

Hunt, J. "The Psychological Development of Orphanage-Reared Infants: Interventions with Outcomes (Teheran)." *Genetic Psychology Monographs* 94 (1976): 177–226.

Hymes, D.H. "The Ethnography of Speaking." In *Anthropology and Human Behavior*, edited by T. Gladwin and W.C. Sturtevant. Washington, DC: Anthropological Society of Washington, Smithsonian Institution, 1962.

———, ed. "The Ethnography of Communication." *American Anthropologist* (December 1964):

———. "Competence and Performance in Linguistic Theory." In *Language Acquisition: Models and Methods*, edited by R. Huxley and E. Ingram. New York: Academic Press, 1971.

Kagan, J., and Moss, H. *Birth to Maturity*. New York: Wiley, 1962.

———; Lapidus, R.; and Moore, N. "Infant Antecedents of Cognitive Functioning: A Longitudinal Study." *Child Development* 49 (1978): 1005–1023.

Kamerman, S., and Kahn, A. *Child Care, Family Benefits, and Working Parents*. New York: Columbia University Press, 1981.

———. "Child Care Services: A National Picture." *Monthly Labor Review* 106 (December 1983): 35–39.

———. "Child Care Services: An Issue for Gender Equality and Women's Solidarity." *Child Welfare* LXIV, 3 (May–June 1985): 259–271.

Karabel, J., and Halsey, A.H., eds. *Power and Ideology in Education*. New York: Oxford University, 1979.

King, R. *All Things Bright and Beautiful: A Social Study of Infants' Classrooms*. New York: Wiley and Sons, 1978.

Kohlberg, L. "A Cognitive-Developmental Analysis of Children's Sex-Role Concepts and Attitudes." In *The Development of Sex Differences,* edited by E.E. Maccoby. Stanford, CA: University Press, 1966.

Kohn, M. *Class and Conformity: A Study in Values.* Homewood: Dorsey Press, 1969.

Lamb, M. "Infant Social Cognition and 'Second-Order' Effects." *Infant Behavior and Development* 1 (1978): 1–10.

Locke, J. *Some Thoughts Concerning Education.* (4th ed.) London: A. and J. Churchill, 1699.

Lorenz, K. "The Companion of the Bird's World." *AUK* 54 (1937): 245–273.

Lubeck, S. *Sandbox Society: Early Education in Black and White America.* London: Falmer, 1985.

Malinowski, B. *Myth in Primitive Psychology.* London: Kegan Paul, 1962.

Malmstad, B.; Ginsburg, M.; and Croft, J. "The Social Construction of Reading Lessons: Resistance and Social Reproduction." *Journal of Education* 165 (1983): 359–373.

McGraw, M. *The Child in Painting.* New York: Greystone Press, 1941.

Mills, C. *The Sociological Imagination.* New York: Oxford University Press, 1959.

Minsky, T. "Advice and Comfort for the Working Mother." *Esquire* (November–December 1984): 153–157.

Montessori, M. *Education for a New World.* Wheaton, IL: Theosophical Publishing House, 1963.

———. *Reconstruction in Education.* India: Theosophical Publishing House, 1968.

———. *Peace and Education.* India: Theosophical Publishing House, 1971.

Osborn, D. *Early Childhood Education in Historical Perspective.* Athens: Education Association, 1972.

Piaget, J. *The Origins of Intelligence in Children.* New York: International University Press, 1952.

———. *Play, Dreams, and Imitation in Childhood.* New York: W. W. Norton and Co., 1962.

———. *Science of Education and the Psychology of the Child.* New York: Orion Press, 1970.

Portnoy, F., and Simmons, C. "Day Care and Attachment." *Child Development* 49 (1978): 239–242.

Ragozin, A.S. "Attachment Behavior of Day-Care Children: Naturalistic and Laboratory Observations." *Child Development* 51 (1980): 409–415.

Reinharz, S. *On Becoming a Social Scientist.* San Francisco, CA: Jossey-Bass, 1979.

Robinson, W.P., and Rackstraw, S. *A Question of Answers. Vol. 1–2.* London: Routledge and Kegan Paul, 1971.

Robinson, W.P. "Where Do Children's Answers Come From?" In *Class, Codes and Control*, edited by B. Bernstein. London: Routledge and Kegan Paul, 1973.

Rousseau, J. Emile. *Or Treatise on Education.* New York: D. Appleton and Co., 1893.

Skinner, B.F. *Science and Human Behavior.* New York: Macmillan, 1953.

———. *Verbal Behavior.* New York: Appleton-Century-Croft, 1957.

Spradley, J. *The Ethnographic Interview.* New York: Holt, Rinehart and Winston, 1979.

Stein, H. (1984). "The Case for Staying Home." *Esquire* (November–December 1984): 142–149.

Turner, G. "Social Class and Children's Language of Control at Age Five and Age Seven." In *Class, Codes, and Control*, edited by B. Bernstein. London: Routledge and Kegan Paul, 1973.

———, and Pickvance, R. "Social Class Differences in the Expression of Uncertainty in Five-Year-Old Children" In *Class, Codes, and Control*, edited by B. Bernstein. London: Routledge and Kegan Paul, 1973.

Ulich, R. *Three Thousand Years of Educational Wisdom.* Cambridge, MA: Harvard University Press, 1954.

von Frisch, K. "Decoding the Language of the Bee." *Science* 185 (1974): 663–668.

Waldman, E. "Labor Force Statistics from a Family Perspective." *Monthly Labor Review* 106 (December 1983): 16–20.

Watson, J. *Behaviorism* (2nd ed.). Chicago, IL: University of Chicago Press, 1930.

Weiser, M. *Group Care and Education of Infants and Toddlers.* St. Louis, MO: C. V. Mosby, 1982.

White, B., and Watts, J. *Experience and Environment: Major Influences on the Development of the Young Child. Vol. 2.* Englewood Cliffs, NJ: Prentice Hall, 1973.

White, B. L. *The First Three Years of Life.* New York: Avon, 1975.

White, B.; Kaban, B.; and Attanucci, J. *The Origins of Human Competence: The Final Report of the Harvard Preschool Project.* Boston, MA: Lexington Books, 1978.

Willis, P. *Learning to Labor: How Working Class Kids Get Working Class Jobs.* New York: Columbia University Press, 1981.

Wolff, P. "Observations on the Early Development of Smiling." In *Determinants of Infant Behavior. Vol. 2,* edited by B. M. Foss. London: Methuen, 1963.

Zimmerman, M. *Musical Characteristics of Children.* Washington, DC: MENC, 1971.